GOD
The Interview

GOD
The Interview

TERRY LANE

an
ABC
BOOK

Published by ABC Books for the
AUSTRALIAN BROADCASTING CORPORATION
GPO Box 9994 Sydney NSW 2001

Copyright © Terry Lane, 1993

First published 1993

National Library of Australia
Cataloguing-in-Publication entry
  Lane, Terry, 1939– .
  God: the interview.

  Bibliography.
  ISBN 0 7333 0242 4.

  1. God – Fiction. I. Australian Broadcasting Corporation. II. Title.
A823.3

Edited by Glenda Downing
Designed by Deborah Brash/Brash Design
Set in 11/13 pt. Baskerville
by Midland Typesetters, Maryborough, Victoria
Printed and bound in Australia by
McPherson's Printing Group
5-1495

CONTENTS

'History records very little in the way of mental
activity on the part of the mass of mankind
except a series of stampedes from affirmative
errors into negative ones and back again.'
GBS—*Back to Methuselah*

'To believe in God is impossible, not to
believe in him is absurd.'
VOLTAIRE

'If God didn't exist we would have to
invent Her. On the other hand, if God did
exist we would have to kill Her.'
LANE

'Backward, turn backward, oh Time in your flight.
Make me a monkey again, just for tonight.'
HARRY BENTON

Warning!

*T*here is a great deal in what follows that will be offensive to those who are content in their traditional religious beliefs and practices. If you are in that category of person then I beseech you, do not read any further. It will only make you unhappy, then you will write angry letters to me and that will make me unhappy.

This book is for those who feel that conventional religion has not answered their existential questions. Not, mind you, that I expect that anyone will find any answers to anything here. This is my own, personal attempt to make sense of life, the universe and everything.

I simply offer this as 'alms for oblivion' as someone once called his autobiography. (I have remembered the title long after I have forgotten the name of the author. That's what happens when your book titles are too clever by half.)

In times past I would probably have been burned at the stake for the heretical views expressed in these pages. There are still people around who feel called to carry on the sterling work of Torquemada and the Spanish Inquisition. If you are such a person and you have read this far I beg you—stop now!

This is how one wireless person came to presume to interview God.

A new friend asked me the questions that persons in my profession are often asked, like: 'Whom did you most enjoy interviewing?' 'Whom would you most like to interview?' And then: 'If you interviewed the Pope what would you ask him?'

Well, I think that if ever I got to interview his holiness I would ask him: 'Who do you think you are?'

Not in an impertinent tone of voice, mind you. This is a serious question. The Bishop of Rome is thought by some to be Christ's special representative on earth. The Vicar of Christ, as one of his epithets has it, actually has the authority to stand in the place of Christ. He has the keys of the Kingdom. He is no ordinary mortal. At least that is the official dogma on the matter. What I would like to know is does the present occupant of the Vatican actually believe that.

Which set me thinking. Why limit myself to the Pope? Why not talk directly to God Herself and see what She has to say on the various subjects which trouble us mortals. Like, where have we come from; what are we supposed to be doing while we're here; where do we go after we die; or, indeed, why do we have to die? The second law of thermodynamics is awesomely depressing and we do everything that we can to prevent its remorseless impact on our own persons. We try our hardest to resist the inevitable decline into entropy and formlessness, but in the end the second law will even get Elizabeth Taylor. No cosmetic surgeon yet born can frustrate the second law of thermodynamics.

(My friend who asked me about the Pope is a cosmetic surgeon.)

So, here I am, about to talk to God. And knowing full well that I am fooling no one. This is all coming from inside my own head. But tell me, where else does God exist? Over the years I have read the words of theologians of this and other times. It seems to me that they are all making it up as they go along and the only ones we should trust are those who admit that all they are doing is talking to themselves. This is an important principle of theology. Only trust those who admit the subjectivity of their exercise.

And run as fast as you can from those who tell you that they really can hear the voice of God, just as clearly as they can hear any human voice.

Those who claim to know with absolute certainty, in an objective sense, what God is thinking or saying are the most dangerous people on earth. They always have been. They fly into a fury when anyone presumes to question their God words. They have inquisitions and crusades and witch-hunts to eradicate the sceptic, the heretic and the infidel. They write creeds, and woe betide the person who refuses to subscribe to them. They define what is orthodox and what is heretical and they excommunicate and anathematise the lucky heretics and burn or drown the not-so-lucky. I do not trust or like those who claim to know for certain what God has said on anything. Quite apart from anything else they are fibbers, because the one thing that we all know for certain is that we know very little about anything, at least when it comes down to what we might call ultimate truths. We have no idea Who or What, if Anything, set off the Big Bang and put the whole universe in motion. We certainly have no idea what the Life Force (which is what George Bernard Shaw called his God) intended. We can only assume that if there is any meaning to it all then somehow or other we are part of the meaning. But so is the little green bug that settles on rose stems and looks for all the world like a rose thorn.

Paul Davies, a physicist with whom I have conversations that only he understands, reckons that there 'is something going on in the universe'. He doesn't know what (or at least he didn't, the last time we talked) but he assumes that conscious life, being the highest form of existence of which we are aware, must have some place in whatever it is that is going on. And that is about that! There is very little more that you can say for certain. The rest must come from your imagination. But we are bound to keep our imaginations under control and not let them ride roughshod over the facts as we know them.

For instance, knowing as we do that the earth is a sphere and the universe goes off in all directions to God only knows where (said with all due reverence) then we can't in good conscience claim to believe in the sorts of things that were perfectly respectable for our ancestors who thought that the earth was flat and that God was 'up there' above the sky putting the stars out for our amusement every night. There is nothing 'up there'. Here is a verse from the *Rubaiyat of Omar Khayyam*:

> And that inverted Bowl we call the Sky,
> Whereunder crawling coopt we live and die,
> Lift not thy hands to It for help—for It
> Rolls impotently on as Thou or I.

Which I take to mean that the system in which we live, which technically speaking has neither up nor down, is a closed system in which things happen according to the ineluctable processes of cause and effect and there is no outside intervention to be expected in this process. I ask God about that later on in the conversation because

I think it is important. We need the courage to face the fact that we can generally anticipate what is going to happen and that's that. There are no miracles.

The big problem in talking with God is that She talks in barely audible whispers. You would think that the Creator of the universe would be a bit on the loud side, but not at all. There is a charming little story to this effect in the first book of Kings. Elijah the prophet is hiding in a cave and . . .

> . . . a great and strong wind rent the mountains, and broke in pieces the rocks before the Lord, but the Lord was not in the wind; and after the wind an earthquake, but the Lord was not in the earthquake; and after the earthquake a fire, but the Lord was not in the fire; and after the fire a still small voice.[1]

Needless to say that was God. And do you know what She asked Elijah? 'What are you doing here Elijah?' And that is the ultimate question which we are all trying to answer. 'What am I doing here?'

Elijah was one of those religious people who believe that they and they alone are still 'very jealous for the Lord, the God of hosts'. It's a common delusion. In fact Elijah probably didn't know any more than the rest of us. He was running on a mixture of superstition, wishful thinking and intuition, which is about as much as any of us can do.

We can forgive him his superstition. He didn't know any better. He didn't know about electricity and plate tectonics so it was a reasonable assumption that all the commotion in the storm and the earthquake must have something to do with the Almighty.

Ignorance was common and understandable in old testament times. Noah, for instance, believed that the rainbow was a sign from God that She would refrain from flooding the place ever again. We know that rainbows are the glorious effect of light passing through the prisms of water in the air and have nothing whatever to do with divine pacts. So superstition, forgivable in the time of Noah or Elijah, is a folly that we may not permit ourselves in the late twentieth century. After all, we are not children.

Wishful thinking is another matter. I want the universe, and in particular my little spark in it, to have some sort of meaning. And intuition is the faculty that convinces us that something, God knows what, is going on here. This doesn't look like an accident. If you stumbled across something as complex and improbable as the universe as you were out walking you would be bound to say: Heavens! Here's an interesting *piece of work*.

And who did the work? Well, here She is, in what we in the media business are vain enough to call 'an exclusive interview'.

Once in conversation I questioned the late, great Manning Clark about the way he wrote such subjective history. He presumed to know what long-dead men and women were thinking when they did this or that. He attributed motives to them as though he were their spiritual confidante. He could not possibly have known so much. His defence was simple and elegant. 'Look on the cover,' he said. 'Note that it says "*Manning Clark's* History of Australia". If you don't like it, write your own!'

In such a spirit I offer Terry Lane's conversation with God. If you don't like it, write your own.

But before we talk I will do what I always do in an interview, set the scene with an introduction. You know the sort of thing: 'With me now is Sir David Attenborough, well-known naturalist, broadcaster and inventor of television snooker . . .'

---

[1] Kings 19:11–12

In the Beginning

With me now is God—well-known Creator of the Universe and the Being credited with the authorship (or at least the inspiration) of the sixty-six books which make up the Bible, considered by Christians to be holy scripture, but not necessarily recognised as such by Jews, Muslims, Buddhists, Confucianists and sundry animists and believers in sacred serpents and so on.

According to the Bible, God created the universe in a six-day working week around about 4004 years before the time of Jesus, who is said to be God's son.

We have a lot of ground to cover in this interview—

no less than creation and subsequent events in their entirety. Which may sound like a lot, but in fact there may be less here than meets the eye.

Good afternoon, God, and thanks for your time . . .

Don't mention it—I've got plenty of it.

Yes, and I'm conscious of the fact that I do not have much of it left—which leads me into my first question, which I hope won't sound petulant. Could You please explain why You made the second law of thermodynamics? You know about that?

Well, of course I do. I know everything. I *am* everything, if I may put it that way. The second law of thermodynamics says that in a system the entropy cannot decrease for any spontaneous process. In fact the entropy of the universe as a whole is tending to maximum. Is that clear?

Not really, but I think that I know what it means in general.

Well, it simply means that everything is running down. Eventually, everything will sort of collapse into an undifferentiated clod. But you shouldn't worry about that, because it won't happen for a long time. Except in your case personally—you're running down now and tending towards maximum entropy. Which is just the way things are because it happens to be a feature of Me.

When I thought the Big Bang and the pre-existing singularity exploded into the observable universe all the things that you call the laws of physics came into being at that moment, because they just happen to be part of Me. In fact, without the operation of the second law of thermodynamics there could not have been a Big Bang. Bangs, by their very nature, involve the operation of the second law. Therefore everything that follows from the Big Bang must also be subject to the law which is inherent in the energy of the explosion itself. So the second law and time and space and matter and gravity and energy all came into being at the same time—because that's just what I'm like.

But I thought that You were like us? What about: 'Then God said, "Let us make man in our image, after our likeness" '?

Let me tell you that the person who wrote those words was a considerable poet, but ignorant and vain beyond belief. Which 'man' did I make in my image? Cro-Magnon man? Neanderthal man? Peking man? Come on—I didn't *make* anything, in the sense of sitting down and designing this or that animal from the genes up.

This could be the hardest thing for you to understand, but I don't *intend* or *will* or *make* anything. I don't deal in intentions. My speciality is possibilities and potentials.

Now I happen to know that you are fascinated by those little green insects that look so much like rose thorns that if they settle on a rose stem they will be safe from birds. They are very amusing little fellows. My favourite amongst the insects travelling in disguise is the stick insect with the two tiny dead leaves on his tail. Now that is what I call design overkill. The stick facsimile is enough. The two little leaves are really gilding the lily.

So. Do you seriously think that I sat down one Thursday morning and said: 'Look, just for a joke, how about I cobble together an insect that looks like a dead stick.' Which I then proceeded to do. But not being One to leave well enough alone I say to Myself: 'Now then—the finishing touch! Voila! Two little facsimile dead leaves on the end of his tail! Wow! Talk about laugh!' And so on . . .

Commonsense tells you that it didn't happen like that, doesn't it? Charles Darwin figured out how that happened and he got it right. Before Darwin you could have been forgiven for thinking that the stick insect was one of my more amusing designs and you could have deduced from it that the Creator has a sense of humour, but after Darwin there is no longer any excuse for ignorance and superstition.

Homo sapiens is no different from the order Phasmida in that respect. Once those sub-microscopic self-replicating entities, the genes, started their quest for immortality they were bound to end up with a myriad different external forms. I certainly didn't design any of the outcomes of the evolutionary process. I just observe what happens. Did you know that the Indian stick insect, *Carausius morosus*, reproduces parthenogenetically? That the male is utterly irrelevant? That's a sobering thought for you. I wonder what he makes of life? Very depressing for him, I should say. But believe me, it was never my intention that it should be that way—but right from the outset it was always *possible* that it would turn out like that.

I mean, take your common aphid, for example. Mother aphid reproduces clones of herself without any male intervention at all. Now that is one very satisfied feminist we have there. She passes on her genes totally undiluted. In one sense you would have to say that she is the most successful form of life on earth. She does much better for herself than humans do. You lot go through a rigmarole that results in a genetic compromise whereby the mother and the father have to lose half their genes each in the process. Not very neat at all.

Are You telling me that Homo sapiens *is no more interesting in the ultimate sense than aphids?*

No, I'm not saying that you are no more interesting— I'm simply saying that in the Creation, if we must call it that, all that I did was to set up endless possibilities. You are just one of the possibilities inherent in the system I set up with the Big Bang. You may find tigers more interesting than aphids, but that is purely an aesthetic judgment and not to be taken at all as a qualitative assessment.

Homo sapiens is more interesting to you because you are part of the species and because you feel that a self-conscious creature with the ability to communicate by language must of necessity be more interesting. No other species can do that, and therefore no other species asks questions about origins and meanings. But believe Me, you are no better or worse in a qualitative sense than the aphids. But I must tell you that they have very limited imaginations.

Inherent in the universe right from the outset was the possibility—but not the inevitability—that one day there would be aphids and there would also be intelligent, conscious life forms that would be curious enough to want to know what the universe consists of and how it holds together and whether or not there is a design or purpose behind it. Did I know what form it would take? Well, yes and no. Given that for Me everything that happens happens in the present, nothing takes me by surprise. But I didn't plan that one day there would be a bifurcated, upright, talking ape who would presume to suggest that he resembles Me. But it is in the nature of the universe itself that such a creature could emerge from exactly the same process of selection and mutation which produced the aphid.

Has it happened anywhere else in the universe?

Oh yes, there are several other spots where intelligent, self-reflective consciousness has evolved.

Are they like us?

Well, yes—in the sense that the intelligent life forms have some things in common. You all tend to walk upright, which I find interesting. Do you know about Jean Baptiste Pierre Antoine de Monet Lamarck? Everybody laughs at Lamarck these days for his theories of the transmission of acquired characteristics from one generation to the next. After all, as the Darwinians say, the giraffe didn't get a long neck by reaching higher and higher until she dislocated her neck and then passed on this characteristic of the dislocated neck to her offspring. But when it comes to walking upright I think we should keep an open mind. It looks like the genetic transmission of an acquired trait. But I digress.

Yes, there are other intelligent life forms in the universe. Not many, mind you—because although the possibility was always there, right from the beginning, the circumstances had to be just right for inorganic molecules to turn the trick of becoming self-replicating, organic molecules. You need very special conditions, even in this best of all possible universes, for genes to start emerging from the mud. And even in a universe of vast size and extraordinary possibilities this is something that is only going to happen a few times.

How many times?

Seven, actually. There are seven planets in all on which this particular phenomenon has occurred.

And they are all like us?

More or less, except for one thing.

What is that?

I have to tell you that nowhere on the other six planets on which there is intelligent life is that life form devoting most of its energies and resources to making itself extinct. This may come as a surprise to you, but it is not an essential characteristic of intelligent life that it should commit so much to technology. And in particular, the technology of mass murder. War is a very interesting phenomenon—you earth creatures are unique in that respect. Perhaps we might talk more about technology later on if that's all right with you, because I find this phenomenon really very interesting. Could we do that?

Certainly. But before we do that I would like You to talk more about what life means if You didn't actually design things the way we see them. I once asked the great naturalist, Sir David Attenborough—You've heard of him . . . ?

Of course.

I asked him if he could see any meaning in life. We had been talking at the time about a frog in South America that lives under a waterfall and, because the noise of the water makes croaking a waste of time, has developed blue feet with which he semaphores his amorous intentions to any lady frog he happens to encounter under the waterfall. This visual croak struck me as being a very interesting adaptation to the frog's peculiarly noisy environment. But it seemed a lot of trouble to go to, developing a bright blue foot just to enhance his copulatory prospects. Is that all it means? Sir David said that he thought that would be as much meaning as the frog would need to be going on with—and if increasing copulatory chances was good enough for the frog then it would have to be good enough for us.

And he's quite right. First and foremost the meaning of life for every single life form in the universe is life. I know that this is considered ideologically unsound in certain quarters these days, but you might as well face the fact that you are born to reproduce—anything else is a bonus. You have no trouble accepting that fact of life for wombats, sparrows and bees, but you humans are too vain to accept that the same rule applies to you. Well, I have news for you. That is why you were born, like it or not. Your parents didn't produce you because they had some plan in mind for their sperm and ova, did they? They copulated and had a baby. Just like the blue-footed frog.

The frog's foot didn't become a vivid blue by either

the frog's intention or Mine. Over many froggy generations the males with bright blue feet did better in the copulatory stakes than those with just a tinge of sky-blue pigment. The brighter the blue the better his chances of being seen and of producing a clutch of tadpoles. This is the biological determinism which seems to trouble some humans so deeply. But wishing it were otherwise will not alter the facts of the matter that characteristics are acquired and reinforced over generations simply because they enhance the survival prospects of the genes of the creature.

You lot have worked out a way to break the nexus between copulation and reproduction, which is very clever and opens up all sorts of possibilities for you. For one thing, you should now be able to avoid breeding yourself out of living space, which will be a good thing. And for another, it means that the functions of males and females needn't be so delimited as it is for other species. But still the genetic imperative is there just as much for you as for stick insects or blue-footed frogs. You live to reproduce.

But you have it all over stick insects and even wombats, because you can imagine other meanings and you can manipulate things to make them come true. But these are artificial meanings, not natural ones. Mind you, that doesn't make them any less important. In fact, it is what makes you interesting as a species. You can now create your own meanings. You don't have to accept the imperatives. This is wonderful for you and interesting for Me. But do you see what it means when you ask: 'What is the meaning of life?'

It means there are two answers. One is the same for you as it is for the blue-footed frog. The meaning of life is *life*. You are a small link in a reproductive chain that has enabled your genes to resist the inexorable forces of the second law of thermodynamics. By the process of reproduction the genes have bought immortality. They are the true survivors. You just get to carry them around.

But the second answer to the question 'What is the meaning of life?' is this: life means whatever you want it to mean. And there is no ultimate, universal answer, applicable to all humans. Everyone has a different meaning. And while at one minute you think you know with absolute certainty what you want out of life, you soon find that the whole matter is subject to trade-offs, bargaining and compromises.

Well, if You want to know what I want out of life the answer is easy. I want to live forever; be fabulously wealthy; have experience sexual ecstasy several times a day; hold a high and respected position in society and never have to work again as long as I live. It's pretty simple and straightforward really.

True—but the fly in the ointment of life is the second law of thermodynamics. You cannot live forever. You are going to run down to nothing sometime before you have lived 100 years, I would think. Let me tell you a story.

A great and wise king once asked his cleverest court philosophers: 'Tell me true, what is the meaning of life?'

One philosopher said immediately: 'Majesty, the meaning of life consists in great wealth. From the day of our birth until the day we die we long for that plenitude of wealth which would free us for all our lives of the tyranny of work. We crave idleness and we endure work only that we not starve.'

The second philosopher replied to the king's question: 'Majesty, that which men seek above all else is honour and esteem in the eyes of others. We long for deference and respect, yet at the same time we wish not to have to defer to others. The truth is, Majesty, that all men want to be in your position.'

The third philosopher told the king: 'Majesty, the meaning of life is in pleasure. We desire nothing so much as constant gratification of the senses. Our lusts and our appetites are insatiable. We would exchange wealth and honour for true and lasting satisfaction of the senses.'

The king took note of the answers he had been given. He had all the wealth that greed could imagine and he wanted for nothing, yet still he felt that life was without meaning. He had wives and concubines without number. His feasts and circuses were legendary. He was honoured by all and was deferred to by the haughtiest of his people. Yet he was troubled. 'Perhaps,' he said, 'I take these things for granted, having been born to them. Yet I suspect that there is something that we value more highly than even wealth, pleasure and deference. I propose a test of the meaning of life.

'Go out into the kingdom and find for me an ordinary young man—perhaps nineteen or twenty years of age. He must be neither rich nor destitute. Neither a scholar nor a dullard. He must not be of high estate, yet he must not be a peasant. He must have every prospect of enjoying an *ordinary* life. Find this young man and bring him to me.'

And they did as the king commanded. They sought the young man who had been so described by the king and in time they found him and brought him to the palace.

The king looked upon the young man and said this: 'Young man, I want to know what is the most important thing of all to you. Is it wealth?'

'Sir,' the young man said, 'I would truly like to be wealthy so that I would never have to work again. That would make me very happy.'

The king said: 'And what of pleasure and the joys of the flesh? Do these things matter to you?'

'Sir, I am constantly troubled by the urging of my loins. Yes, indeed, to satisfy my lusts would be a great joy to me.'

'And your station in life—are you quite satisfied with it?'

'Well, to be frank with you, no. I resent having to pay respects to men and women whom I do not admire for either their goodness or their intellect. It seems most unjust that by an accident of birth it is I who should be tugging the forelock to those I deem unworthy of this respect. I should like very much a title and a station in life.'

The king thought for a moment and then said to the young man: 'Very well. All of this can be arranged, if these are the things that would truly make you happy.

'You will from this day be a rich man. From the royal treasury you shall be paid such a sum of money that you will not have to work again.'

The young man was very pleased.

'Also, from today you shall be a Lord of my realm. You shall wear the finest clothes and the highest badges of honour. I shall decree that all who see you are to bow low and address you with due respect and reverence. Does this please you?'

'Oh, indeed. This makes me very happy. I shall be rich and of high estate?'

'Yes. And furthermore, it is in my power to see that you travel only in the finest vehicles and that you wear nothing but the most glorious clothes. You shall not have to wear the same clothes twice. The house in which you will live will be second in magnificence only to my own. Does this also please you?'

'Yes sir.'

'To make the point most clearly that your station is above all others you must call me by my first name and must not under any circumstance use forms of address which are deferential. Is that understood?'

'Thank you Cyril, I take you at your word. Now what about the satisfying of my lusts?'

'On that score you shall have no complaints. The fairest maids in all the land shall minister to your senses. Or, if not maids, then beautiful boys if that is your preference. It is entirely up to you. Whomever you choose they shall be instructed in the arts of love and will know how to lift a man into the highest halls of ecstasy. Is this to your liking?'

'I could not ask for more. I am ecstatic in anticipation. But I cannot believe that all this will come without a price. There must be something that you want in return. What, pray you, is your price?'

The king looked closely into the eyes of the young man and said, very quietly: 'In one year I want your life.'

'I beg your pardon. In what sense do you mean that you want my life?'

'In one year—after you have enjoyed all that your heart desires for 365 days—you will be killed. It will be done without any pain, I assure you. You will die in complete peace after having enjoyed one whole year of your chosen bliss. Is this not fair?'

'And if I refuse?'

'Well then, of course you are free to go. I will hold no grudge against you. You will have answered my question in part. Next time I am wondering what is the most important thing in life I will know that bliss is important, but to live one year and a day is more important. So how do you choose?'

'Well, if you don't mind I would rather not. Thank you. I will be going now, if you will excuse me.'

The king raised his hand. 'Not so fast young man. Let me change my offer so that you will enjoy all the things you desire for five whole years, rather than one. And on the last day of the fifth year you shall die peacefully and without pain. Now will you take my offer?'

The young man took a moment to reflect on what he was being offered. Five years of sensual delights such as few men could possibly enjoy, and then certain death.

'No. No thank you. I think I should be going.'

'Ten years, then,' the king said.

The young man thought a little longer. He was tempted. But again he refused. The king increased his offer to twenty, then thirty, then forty years. Finally, he said: 'My last offer to you is that you should live as you desire for eighty years and then die peacefully but unnaturally. How do you choose?'

The young man thought. In eighty years he would be 100 years of age. What did he have to lose from such an agreement. It was unlikely that he should live to such an age.

'I accept,' he said. 'When do I begin?'

The king shook his head.

'I am sorry,' he said, 'but I am withdrawing my offer. You have answered my question. Had you accepted one year of bliss in return for your life then I would have known that wealth, status and the satisfaction of the senses give life its meaning. Even had you accepted forty years and the certainty of death at sixty I could have drawn from this an inference about the things that give meaning to life. But in the end you have shown me that the meaning of life is life itself. Above all else you wanted to simply go on living. You would give up all that I had offered you for another day of living, even living in poverty and frustration. But thank you, young man, for helping me answer these questions. You may go in peace.'

The young man turned to go, but then he turned back to the king and said: 'Could we backtrack a little and discuss the fifty year option again?'

And what am I supposed to make of that?

Simply that first and foremost the meaning of life is life. It is *not to die*. Then, having chosen to live for as long as possible, you have to choose how you are going to fill in your time until the inevitable comes to pass.

That's not very profound.

No, but what else can it be? It could be that this life is utterly meaningless and that humans have to endure the special torment of knowing that it is all pointless, so why go on with it? Why put up with all the pain

and disappointment—the 'slings and arrows of outrageous fortune that flesh is heir to'—if in the end it
amounts to nothing?

On the other hand, what if the conventionally religious
people are right and this life is a preparation for the
next and if you want to get a comfortable berth in heaven
then you had better be careful how you behave on earth?
Do you believe that?

No.

Then what else can there be in the way of meaning?
Meaning is whatever you make it mean right here and
now.

And what's more the meaning of life may be different
from day to day. Imagine if you were tired of life itself
and thinking of ending it all—something that only
Homo sapiens seems to do, incidentally—what might
make you put it off? Any number of things. You might
have a book to write or a painting to paint or the
shopping to do or the Matterhorn to see or a sick friend
to look after or the cat to feed or someone with whom
to make love—and so on, ad almost infinitum. The
meaning of life is whatever it is that you plan to do
next. And when you run out of things to do and there
is no real reason to get out of bed tomorrow because
there are no more meanings, then you might as well
finish it all. But, of course, it could always be that something will take you by surprise. I have known people
to be so fascinated by the anatomy of a stick insect that
it gave them reason enough to go on living for another
whole day. And why not?

Mind you, if you think that stick insects are small
beer and that only writing ninth symphonies counts as
sufficient reason to go on living then you're in some
sort of trouble. But don't come to me for help. I don't
care.

That's a terrible thing to say—that You don't care . . .

Oh come on. You don't seriously expect Me to take an interest in every human who is bored with life? Or even seriously uninterested in it? Let me put this to you bluntly—there is a God: viz *Me*. And I don't care. Can't you deduce that just by looking around you? It's as plain as the nose on your face.

But every religion is based on the notion that there is a God and that You care.

Not every religion. This is a very Middle Eastern idea that history is a stage on which I act. Well, it's not. History is a sequence of events in which things happen, more or less as one damned thing after another, and none of it makes any sense and you can't hold Me responsible for any of it. Believe Me, if I were running it it would be a lot nicer, but that's not the way My universe works. I'm no more into controlling events than I am into inventing species. History, like the universe, is a sequence of possibilities. I intend or will nothing.

In the fourteenth century it was suggested by Pope Clement that the plague came to Europe 'by a mysterious decree of God'. But you know that some things, like the Black Death, just happen. I didn't infect the fleas and then put them on the rats and send them to Europe. There's no point in flagellating yourself and carrying on with all that *Danse Macabre* stuff. It doesn't impress Me. You have to work out for yourself that hygiene is the key to eradicating the bubonic plague. You know that the plague neither came to Europe nor eventually subsided because of a miracle. Miracles only ever occur where there is ignorance. Because the people of four-teenth century Europe didn't know about fleas and germs their ignorance is understandable, but it would be unforgivable if anyone today were to ascribe an epidemic to Me or the Devil.

I know that superstitious people have a tendency to interpret historical events as My rewards, punishments, warnings or tests for virtues or misdemeanours, as the case may be. In Old Testament times I was supposed to be constantly using Assyrians or Egyptians or frogs, flies or locusts as instruments of punishment for inflicting pain on My 'chosen people' when they went off whoring after false gods.

Honestly now—do I strike you as so petty? I mean, if someone tells you that they prefer to listen to another wireless station would you punish them for their infidelity with a bad case of leprosy?

Well . . .

Most of the Old Testament is a terrible slur on my character—and what makes it all particularly annoying is that I am supposed to have written this stuff about Myself!

Would you like to talk about these things called miracles?

Yes, I would. But first I would like to pick up on something You were saying a minute or two ago about humans breaking the nexus between copulation and reproduction. I had heard that You took strong exception to us doing this.

Who says that?

I think that You know the answer to that. The Bishop of Rome is quite explicit on this—he says that You have decreed that we shouldn't use contraceptives to frustrate Your will because it is unnatural.

I have heard about this peculiar notion. Good Me! What is 'natural'? It is not natural that you humans should live more than twenty-seven years. I had always figured that as the natural life expectancy of your species. Well, you've fixed that.

Talking on a wire over great distances is not natural— and talking through the air over great distances is even more unnatural. Escalators, televisions, painless dentistry and heavier than air flying machines are most certainly unnatural—yet as far as has come to My attention the Bishop of Rome does not eschew these unnatural practices and devices. Surely I hardly need to tell you that the thing that distinguishes you lot from the aphids and blue-footed frogs is your ability to transcend and frustrate nature at every turn. No doubt someone will one day come up with a blue rose and a red budgie—what will his holiness have to say about that?

I'll tell you what is unnatural. To kill people at such a great distance that you can't even see who or what you are killing—that is unnatural. But I note that it happens every day on your planet and as far as My records show the Bishop of Rome has never once put on his peculiar hat, sat on his throne and made an ex-cathedra pronouncement to the effect that I am mightily perplexed that a creature claiming to be intelligent should commit these unnatural acts. If the bishop thinks that I am fussed about the fate of a sperm or an ovum while turning a celestial blind eye to the deaths of millions of living, breathing, desperately-wanting-to-live fully fledged human beings then he must have a very low opinion of Me.

Whenever I tune into what's going on down there all I seem to get is sex, sex, sex. And those who claim to speak on My behalf are very presumptuous—making the quite erroneous assumption that I care about who does it with whom and in what marital state or not.

Does it not strike you as very odd that the churches have made many definitive rulings about sex over the centuries but have been relatively silent on the subjects of war, economic exploitation, slavery, torture, capital punishment and so on. I know that these days there are a few bolshie parsons and bishops having things to say on the subjects that really matter, but My Me, it's taken a long time to get around to it.

Let Me put this as plainly as I possibly can. Sexual reproduction was not something that I dreamed up in some celestial R & D laboratory. Sexual reproduction developed as a trick used by some species—not all, let

Me emphasise again—to protect themselves from parasites. By altering your genetic composition every generation you outsmart all sorts of viruses and parasites that
would otherwise latch onto you and wipe you out in
no time. Sexual reproduction, resulting as it does in a
constantly changing genetic make-up makes it harder
for the freeloaders to adapt and get a foothold.

Now, tell Me, why should I care what happens in
the process of sexual reproduction? For you it may be
a big deal—I believe that you may even feel the earth
move on occasion. And therefore you may feel that it
is the single most important thing that can happen to
you, which in a way it is. But why should it impress
Me? Why should I lay down rules governing the proper
place, time, partner and intention for copulation? It is
a preposterous notion.

If you want to make rules about such an important
activity then that is your business, but don't hold Me
responsible. If his holiness wants all his followers to
forswear the condom and the pill then that's between
him and them. If he reckons that only married couples
should do it and that auto-eroticism can send you blind
then that is his problem. Although just as a simple
practical problem it would be interesting to know how
he intends to keep track of all those little wrigglers and
make certain that none comes to a useless end and that
they all find their mark.

Are You male or female?

Good grief! Is that a serious question? You want to know
if the ineffable, infinite, eternal, omnipotent creative
spirit is a bloke or a woman? I take it that you are joking?

*Not at all—many people take this very seriously. They
say that You are a man and that therefore women are,
by definition, not fit to be priests, because they are not
the same sex as You.*

A man? What is a man? A hairless ape, distinguished

from the other hairless ape called 'woman' by some dingly-danglies between the legs? Would you like to take a peek in God's holy trousers, perhaps?

You don't seem to be taking this very seriously . . .

How in heaven's name can I take it seriously? How many times do I have to tell you that I am not a human analogue? Or, to put it more properly, you are not a God analogue. I most definitely did *not* make you in My image. But I will say this—since the only thing that really matters to you about Me is that I actually gave birth to the universe you would have to say, that in the only significant feature of My divine self that approximates any human characteristic, I am female. Of course, if you prefer to think of Me as a combination of boss, judge and field marshal then I am a male.

Look, the male/female dichotomy only makes sense in talking about a creature which reproduces by sexual congress. What are these 'God is a male' lot suggesting?

You mean that You are an It? That sounds too rude . . .

Well, you can call Me Cliff if you must have a handle for Me.

But You just said that You are not male.

Oh, all right—Penelope then.

I'm not sure that 'Our Penelope who art in heaven, hallowed be Thy name' will catch on. Or 'Our Cliff' either, for that matter.

Possibly not—but it does tend to emphasise how stupid and infantile it is to ascribe human characteristics to Me, doesn't it? 'Our Father' sounds just as silly to Me as 'Our Cliff'. Why not pick up Shaw's name for Me? How about 'Our Life Force'? You could really make something out of that if you put your mind to it. It has a nice euphonious quality and it is sufficiently abstract to avoid any anthropomorphic misconceptions.

You are no doubt aware of the fact that sexual repro-duction is getting us into all sorts of trouble these days with the females claiming that they have been getting the rough end of the stick for the past four billion years. Do You have any advice on this matter?

Human beings are terrible whingers, aren't you? I mean, I don't hear the blue-footed frog whining about having to take care of the eggs. The gentleman seahorse is not constantly on the hot line to heaven wanting to know why he has to carry the sea colts and fillies around in his shirt while Mrs Seahorse is off overseeing corporate mergers or felling forest giants. The rest of creation—if I may presume to call it that—just gets on with doing what comes naturally.

Now, as you lot have so comprehensively outfoxed nature it is not inconceivable that you might go in for a bit of gender role reversal—but be warned. The genes are not lightly mocked! For four billion years a division of labour has evolved which has suited your genes down to the ground because it has provided the best chance for survival. But you are now the agents of your own evolution—so you can choose for yourself how you want to go from here on, but there are a lot of urges built into those genes that won't go away without putting up a fight.

Women tend to get very testy about any suggestion of biological determinism. They reckon that there is no such thing.

Tell that to the aphids! Of course there is such a thing as biological determinism. Without it your species would not exist. If you had not evolved the behaviour best suited to guarantee survival in your environment then your species would have disappeared. Predators would have had you for breakfast millennia ago. Of course you don't want to hear the unpalatable truth—but the combin-ation of maternal instinct in women and the instinct to fight and copulate in men has best suited your survival prospects. Women are programmed to bear and care for babies—men are programmed to be horrible to women and to each other. But you are not the first species to modify behaviour which guaranteed survival in the past but now threatens survival in the future. However, you are the first species ever to be able to perceive this fact and do something about it by an act of will, rather than waiting for the slow processes of selection to effect the changes.

Will You help?

Of course not. From a purely selfish point of view I might find that the extinction of *Homo sapiens* leads to a much more interesting replacement with an altogether less childish apprehension of things. Shaw reckoned that '. . . the power that produced Man when the monkey was not up to the mark can produce a higher creature than Man if Man does not come up to the mark.' It's crudely put, but his heart's in the right place. I am a disinterested (but not uninterested) observer, not a meddler. You are on your own.

That's a bleak way of putting it?

Bleak it may be, but has anything ever happened that you have observed that suggests that it could be any other way? Have you ever seen any evidence of an outside Force saving humans from the consequences of your own folly? All recorded human history is the story of one damned folly after another. There is no evidence in history that you are getting any help from outside, is there? You are on your own down there—and the sooner you grasp that fact the better.

There are no miracles?

There are no miracles. None. Never. To put that matter beyond argument and speculation let me set you straight once and for all on the matter of miracles. How are your batteries?

· 2 ·

Miracles

*N*ow, *You have volunteered to set us straight on miracles—You say that there are no such things.*

Before we start talking about miracles let's agree on a definition—otherwise we will be floundering around arguing about events which are really just inexplicable with your present knowledge.

No doubt, as I have said, there were people in fourteenth century Europe who thought that it was a miracle when the Black Death abated for a while. We know that it was just that the rats had gone into decline for some reason. So we need a watertight definition of a miracle so that we can't go slipping around in illogical arguments.

Would You care to define a miracle for us then?

Yes, I will. A miracle must be an event which cannot now, or ever, be explained as a natural occurrence or phenomenon. There must be no explanation for it other than intervention from outside the natural order of the universe. There must be no physical, chemical or other way of accounting for this event for it to qualify as a miracle.

Now, it so happens that turning water into wine qualifies under this definition. This is pure magic. There can be no possible chemical explanation for the transformation of H_2O into wine. But we don't know enough about this event to be able to say with certainty that it ever happened. Indeed, the evidence for this miracle is so flimsy that we can say that we are not obliged to take it seriously. Some person, devout, no doubt, but misguided, has seen fit to retail this little story which can now neither be proved nor disproved. Perhaps it was never intended to be taken literally, but rather is an allegory which stands for something else. Anyway, commonsense tells us that it never happened for the simple and sufficient reason that it is impossible. So if we are to talk sensibly about miracles we need a contemporary miracle which can be tested rationally.

These days miracles are not as common as they once were because you don't need them as much. A couple of hundred years ago you needed miracles to cure smallpox or you died. More recently, you needed a miracle to get better from poliomyelitis. These days you have vaccinations, so miracles are no longer required.

Here is an interesting aside. In 1829 Pope Leo XII forbade smallpox vaccination because he reckoned that I sent the disease as some sort of divine retribution and it would be an affront to Me to try to thwart its effects.

In fact medical science has shrunk the area in which miracles can, or need to, happen until it is so small that it no longer has to be taken seriously. Once there was enormous scope for miracles; today there is a tiny corner of ignorance in which the superstitious can fall back on miracles for assistance or explanation of the inexplicable.

Penicillin obviated the need for millions of miracles. So miracles are now pretty much confined to the cancer area because that's the one zone of ignorance left in which miracles can be given room to happen. People sometimes get surprising remissions from cancer—bingo! It is declared a miracle. The doctors are astonished. They expected the patient to be dead by Thursday and here she is up and about, not a trace of malignancy in her system. God must have done it, there can be no other explanation.

Now let me tell you why I, as God, find it very offensive rather than flattering to be given the praise for a surprising cure. This is a moral issue we are dealing with here, more than a metaphysical one. You can argue all you like about what I may or may not be able to do when I am in the mood, but ultimately you have to deal with the ancient conundrum:

If God is omnipotent, then She can't be good.
If God is good, then She can't be omnipotent.

You see, this is a moral riddle, not a religious one. If I *can* cure one cancer then I *ought* to cure all cancers. To pick and choose which I will cure and which I will ignore is immoral.

Think about this. You are standing by a lake. A small child is drowning. You are an adequate swimmer. It is no trouble for you to jump in and save the child. In fact the lake is so shallow that although it is deep enough to drown a child you can wade to the child's rescue. What is your moral obligation in that situation?

I would have to save the child . . .

Exactly. At no risk to yourself you *can* save the child's
life, therefore there is no question that you *ought* to
save the child's life. It is the simplest moral equation
imaginable. Now consider My position.

Some people claim that I have cured their cancer. The
doctor has declared them past medical help. He has
advised that if they want to re-read *Gone with the Wind*
or if they have a Mahler symphony they want to hear
one last time then they should get started right now.
There is not a moment to lose. Then lo! The cancer,
for some reason that medical science cannot explain, goes
away. And scientific ignorance is an excuse to fall back
on the old superstition. It must be a miracle!

But it is clear that if I *can* save the life of one person
with cancer then I *ought* to save the lives of all cancer
sufferers. It's no good saying that I am God, therefore
I can pick and choose to do whatever I like. You had
no choice but to save the drowning child. You were under
an imperative to do what you could do. Am I *less than
human*? Do I live by some moral principle that is
ethically offensive to humans but can somehow be
excused on the grounds of ineffable mystery or whatever?
This is a ridiculous proposition. Morality is an indi-
visible concept. We know what is right—and what we
know to be correct behaviour for mortals cannot be less
true for gods, can it?

*I talked to a man the other day who says that he has
'a walking, talking relationship' with You.*

'Walking, talking'? Did he say that?

*Those were his exact words—heard by thousands as he
said them on this very wireless program.*

I see. And while we were walking and talking what did
I say to him?

Actually the man in question told me that You had been

talking to him about the cause of his cancer, which You had miraculously cured.

I did?

That's right. He said to me that when he discovered that he had the cancer he 'got to talking with God, Who is now My Father, and I said to Him "Lord, how come I was afflicted with this cancer, when Your word says that not a sparrow falls without Your knowledge. Which means that it is with Your permission that this has entered me." '

Well, what a very interesting idea. I gave the cancer 'permission' to go ahead?

Actually the story gets a bit confusing at this point. Because in the next breath he told me that he was afflicted by the 'Evil one'—so I presume that he means that You gave the Devil the OK to go ahead and do his worst.

Really. And why, pray, did I enter into this agreement with the Devil?

I assumed that You would be able to explain it to me. After all, You and he are supposed to have discussed this at some length. The man told me that while he was wondering himself why You would have done this that the Holy Spirit came along and showed him what he had done that had got him offside with Your Almightyship.

It must have been something really terrible that I should punish him like this, wouldn't you say?

Well, absolutely. But he told me that 'He (that's You) showed me areas of questionable integrity . . . He even showed me an income tax return that I had filed a couple of years back which was not really accurate.'

I take it that you are pulling My leg?

No, no! Cross my heart. Every one of these words is

exactly what he said to me. And he was quite adamant that it was You who reminded him of these sins and misdemeanors.

Now let me get this straight. Here is a man in the pink of health and suddenly the Devil says: 'Come on, let me have a go at him. Just a little cancer. Go on—be a Sport.'

You did it with Job.

That, as you well know, is pure fiction. Anyway, I must have said to Myself—well, this bloke did fiddle his tax return a couple of years ago. So why not? And I tell the Devil: Go for it. But if he says he's sorry then we call the cancer off. Is that the way I did it?

Well, yes. I suppose that in purely human terms that is what You must have done.

Did he get in touch with tax department to pay up what he owed?

I don't know. He didn't say. But I suppose that he must have, because You made him better. He told me that 'God kept His word to me. He healed me and delivered me from that cancer.'

Tell me something. Children don't even file tax returns. What do you suppose that they get up to that is so offensive to Me that I give the Devil the OK to hit them with leukemia? Or cot death?

I asked him about that.

And what did he say?

'And for that child there's healing too, in Jesus' name.'

Do you know what that means?

I have no idea. I assume that You must know what it means. It reminded me of a Jesus story in one of the gospels. Jesus was walking amongst the blind and lame

one day when he came upon a man who had been blind
from birth. Now if you believe that illness is punishment
for sin then you are bound to find congenital handicaps
a bit of a puzzle. So his disciples asked him . . .

> 'Rabbi, who sinned, this man or his parents, that he was
> born blind?' Jesus answered, 'It was not that this man sinned,
> or his parents, but that the works of God might be made
> manifest in him.' (John 9:1–3)

Are you telling Me that I made a person to be born
blind so that one day someone would be abe to use him
to do a trick that would reflect well on Me and enhance
My reputation?

I think that is the general idea, yes.

And what about all those people who are born blind but
don't happen to be at the right spot when Jesus is passing?
   Congenital blindness is usually caused by german
measles during pregnancy, isn't it? And have you not
just about eradicated that disease amongst pregnant
women? Which means that you are interfering with My
divine scheme to arrange for a certain number of congenitally blind people to be on hand, just in case the
need comes over Me to pass a miracle. You had better
be careful—I might get cross, and a cross God has been
known to hit, and hit hard, with locusts and plagues.

You are joking, aren't You?

Just look at what you are suggesting. A man gets cancer.
He reckons that I let him have it because he fiddled
his tax return. So he pays up and gets better.
   Problem number one. Millions of people fiddle their
tax returns. Most probably don't even get found out by
the taxation department, let alone struck by cancer.
   Problem number two. Millions of people get cancer,
including small children. Most of them are as honest
as the day is long.

Problem number three. Is cancer a fair and fitting punishment for tax dodging?

Problem number four. If we are going to make cancer the statutory punishment for tax evasion shouldn't we put a warning at the top of the tax return form letting people know what's in store for them if they fudge the figures to their advantage?

Problem number five. How am I going to punish the tax dodgers after you've worked out a cure for cancer? Give them a Divine shove under a bus, perhaps?

Problem number six. Are you stupid or something?

Look, I don't know. I suppose that he didn't mean that You give every tax evader cancer. He just meant himself in particular.

Yes, but don't you see that even by human standards punishment should be consistent. It should fit the crime. It should not be arbitrary. It should not be cruel. Can't you see that even by miserable *human* standards this bloke is describing a moral monster. Do you think that I am actually morally *inferior* to humans?

No, not inferior—just different.

Hey, come on. When you start talking morals you are not talking about taste in clothing. A person who uses torture to extract a confession from a prisoner is not just morally *different* from the humane person who condemns torture. He is morally *worse*. You cannot escape the qualitative judgment on the person.

So when you propose that I act in a way which is morally repulsive to humans then you are not saying that I am merely *different*.

If you really believe that I can *do miracles* on some sort of divine whim then you are saying that I am personally responsible for every deformed baby that I allowed to be born; or for every airliner that crashes; every drought and famine; every earthquake and volcano; every death camp and every smart bomb that seeks out the warmth of human bodies and flies unerringly down the airshaft to vaporise hundreds of women and children.

People have believed that over the years. They have been prepared to take the good divine intervention with the bad and interpret everything that happened to them as somehow My doing. The authors of the book of Joshua believed precisely that. They told a fanciful tale about Me making the sun and moon stand still to give the invading Israelites time to kill all the defending Amorites before tea time. I should sue! Do you believe in that sort of destructive miracle?

What the miracle-believers say about Me is that I *can* keep airliners up, or I *can* stop volcanoes going off, or rivers overflowing their banks, or cholera germs spreading, but for some obscure and ultimately impenetrable reason I don't. Just as easily as you could wade through shallow waters—indeed, more easily and more safely— I could prevent every human tragedy, but I choose not to. What sort of God is that?

At the risk of boring you with repetition, let me say again that the notion of Me *doing* things is infantile. It is an offence to science, reason and morality. It keeps theologians up at night pondering questions like: Why do good people suffer? Why do the wicked prosper? Why do I make the sun rise on the good and the evil and the rain fall on the just and the unjust? They are truly stupid questions which will only be asked by those suffering under the delusion that I take a direct interest in the movement of the sun or the dispersal of precipitation.

So what does that mean? If there's nothing in it for you in the way of rewards or punishment will you choose to be evil rather than good? Unjust rather than just? Let's face it, most people don't give Me a thought when they are choosing between possible courses of action. You choose to do good rather than evil for purely pragmatic reasons, not to amuse Me. Because, generally speaking, it pays to do what you call 'good'. Even at some risk to yourself it pays to rescue the drowning child because it is a good principle by which to live, that there is an agreed obligation to rescue drowning children.

When the television reporters ask you how you feel to be a hero and why did you do it, what will you say? Will you say: 'Because God told me to?' Or will you say: 'I *could*, therefore I had to. And, in any case, something embedded deeply in my genes makes me act against my own immediate interests but in the wider interests of the species as a whole.' Tell that to the six o'clock news person and it will probably finish up on the cutting room floor in the 'incomprehensible' pile, but it is the truth.

We'll talk some more later on about good and evil and why you make a distinction between good and evil deeds which no other species bothers to make.

So there are no miracles? We cannot expect any help from outside the system?

That's right. The greatest disservice that religion has done to humanity since the time that Francis Bacon laid down the principle of scientific inquiry has been to labour mightily to keep superstition and ignorance triumphant over knowledge and reason. It is hard to think of a single advance in knowledge from Copernicus to Darwin that the Churches have not opposed. This aversion to truth is one of the most astonishing phenomena of history which can probably only be understood if we consider that each piece of new knowledge tended to undermine dogma.

Copernicus and Galileo recognised that the earth is not the centre of the universe which, if true, would make nonsense of the claim that I have a special interest in your planet. When Galileo admitted in 1632 that he was persuaded by the heretical Copernican theory the full force of the Inquisition was turned against him and, very prudently, when he was threatened with torture, he recanted and affirmed that the sun did indeed orbit about the earth and that the earth was the centre of the universe—beyond all doubt!

Do you know that in 1979 the Vatican set up a commission to inquire into the 'Galileo affair'—as if there was anything to inquire into! I mean, what if they had decided that he had got it wrong and that when the Pope says the sun revolves around the earth, then that is the last word on the matter? In 1992 the commission made its report and the Roman Church at last got around to forgiving Galileo for his audacity—not to mention heresy—in shoving the earth from the centre to the periphery of the universe. It's hard to know which is more amazing, the ability of the Church to hold a grudge or its refusal to face up to cosmic facts. Or that it should have the effrontery to forgive Galileo rather than going in shame into the public arena to beg for forgiveness itself.

It's a bit like the Vatican's recent decision to remove a reference to the 'perfidious Jew' from its liturgy and then expecting everyone to admire its generosity of spirit.

While Copernicus and Galileo pushed human beings from the physical centre to the edge of the universe, Charles Darwin forced humans to face their common origins with all living species, raising the question: How could God be interested in humans if you are no more special in your origins than a stick insect?

An interesting consequence of the Church's defence of ignorance is that, as the power of the church has declined and science has gained in influence, so the Church has been seen as more and more ridiculous the harder it fought to defend its indefensible cosmology. What makes this all the more interesting is the realisation that if the Church had been able to assert its totalitarian will without challenge then humans today would know nothing of astronomy, evolution, chemistry, physics or medicine. If it *could* have done so the Church would have enforced ignorance for all time.

There are Christians who argue that the Church only

opposed the extension of knowledge because that was what everyone was doing at the time. You know, like the Church only supported slavery or went to war or hunted witches or burned Jews and dissenters because that is what everyone did at the time. Well, take it from Me, that is not true. There was a special, intrinsic quality in the Christian Church which made it particularly hostile to truth. We might talk more about that later on if that's all right with you.

Of course. But first could we talk about Jesus and his alleged 'special relationship' with You?

Certainly.

· 3 ·

Jesus

*T*alking about Jesus and his relationship with You *is very dangerous. Millions of people have been murdered one way or another for not getting the formula just right. The first Christian to be murdered by other Christians was the Spaniard Priscillian. The bishops had him be-headed in 385 because he didn't subscribe to the right formula for the Trinity. And he also didn't believe that Jesus rose from the dead. I guess he was asking for trouble.*

Anyway, do we have to take Jesus as a phenomenon in its entirety—virgin birth, miracles, resurrection,

40

ascension and special Sonship—or can we pick and choose, having the humane teachings without the fairy story?

In the final analysis, whether you take any notice of what Jesus said has nothing whatever to do with the purported manner of his birth, the fact that he turned water into wine or that he was supposed to have walked on water or returned from the dead. Ultimately, you either believe what he said because it makes sense or you disbelieve because it seems like nonsense.

And as for some claim to be 'the son of God'—that validates nothing. And in any case, Jesus said that anyone could qualify for the epithet 'son of God'. He singled out peacemakers for special attention. Remember? 'Blessed are the peacemakers, for they shall be called sons (and daughters, of course) of God.'

What do you think of those words? Good, aren't they? And they get their authority from their inherent good sense, not from some spurious claim to divinity by the author.

Let's put the case another way. I want you to imagine that you've never heard of a person called Jesus. You know absolutely nothing about him. The name has never been mentioned to you. You are 100 per cent ignorant about this man. I know that this intellectual exercise is not easy. Your memory banks are full of stories about Jesus which you think you remember—but in fact if you were to sit down and read the gospels right through from beginning to end in one sitting you might be surprised at how selective the Church has been in retailing the information contained in them. But let's leave that for the moment. Are you ready for me to tell you about this man, of whom you have never heard?

Well, yes, I suppose so . . .

Good. Here we go.

Good afternoon, Mr Lane. It's a lovely day today. I

say, have you heard about this Jesus of Nazareth fellow they're all talking about?

No—what about him?

Well, you won't believe this, but they say that he was born by some miraculous method from a woman who had never ever had sexual intercourse. Is that not astonishing? A virgin birth. I thought that only aphids and stick insects could do that.

Mr Lane, you're smirking. This is perfectly serious stuff I am telling you here. You are looking sceptical. Just wait till I tell you the rest. This Jesus chap went to a wedding and when the wine ran out he called for a jug of water and turned it into wine. The guests said that it was the best vintage that the host had served all day. How about that?

Mr Lane, you're smirking again. Jesus did much more than that. He cursed a fig tree that didn't have any fruit on it out of season and it died. Is that not a peculiar and bad-tempered thing to do? Then he resuscitated his friend Lazarus who had been dead for days. He performed ophthalmological miracles on the blind and did astonishing things for the cripples, like making them walk which they hadn't done for years. What's more, he drove out demons . . .

He what?

He drove demons from people. There were these people, you see, who had terrible hallucinations and could be quite violent and a danger to themselves and to others. They had demons inside them making them behave in this antisocial way, and Jesus used to say to these demons: 'Go away . . .' and sometimes they—the demons, that is—would get out of the people and get into pigs and the pigs would run down into the lake and drown.

Look, I don't mean to be rude, but this condition You describe is obviously schizophrenia and it has nothing

*to do with demons. It's probably organic in origin and
all this demon business is mere superstition.*

Exactly My point. Now, imagine that I have told you
all this and more besides. In the end Jesus is executed,
but after a couple of days he comes back to life and
then, after a few more days, he flies up to heaven. You
see, I can tell from the look on your face that you don't
believe any of it.

And now if I tell you that this same Jesus once said:
'Blessed are the merciful, for they shall obtain mercy,'
how do you react? Do you say: 'Well, a chap who's done
so many miracles must know a thing or two.' Or do
you say: 'Why are these beautiful words buried in this
totally incredible story? Already I am prejudiced against
this Jesus fellow because of the fairytales about miracles
and demons and virgin births—yet the words have true
humane wisdom in them.'

You see the point that I am making? Far from lending
artistic verisimilitude to an otherwise bald and uncor-
roborated narrative, the miracle stories actually prejudice
you against the man who says: 'Blessed are those who
hunger and thirst for righteousness, for they shall be
satisfied.' And that's a terrible shame.

You don't need to believe that the author of words
like these is the son of God to get a kick from them.
'Consider the lilies of the field, how they grow; they
neither toil nor spin; yet I tell you, even Solomon in
all his glory was not arrayed like one of these.' Beautiful,
is it not? But for people who believed that the earth
was flat and that mental illness was caused by demons
resident in the sufferer's system there was an irresistible
urge to gild the lily, as it were. A miracle here and there
would prove beyond doubt that this man spoke with
special authority. And then, just to put the matter beyond
any doubt, let's call him 'the son of God' and then dare
anyone not to take him seriously.

Well, you know what happened. Terrible arguments

ensued between those who believed that Jesus was 'of one substance' with Me and those who, on the other hand, could bring themselves to say no more than that we were 'of like substance'. There were wars and burnings and rackings over that little theological nicety, I can tell you. It was a toss-up who were the more savage, the *homo-ousionists* or the *homoi-ousionists* (that's what they called themselves), but certainly neither wanted in enthusiasm when it came to stamping out heresy by whatever painful method their imaginations could conceive. And so it has gone on.

And the really peculiar thing, as I see it from My particular vantage point in the scheme of things, is that they fought each with such sadistic enthusiasm over these fine points of fanciful metaphysics, all the while completely ignoring the essence of Jesus's ideas.

And what do You think these are?

Well, simple things like how happy are the peacemakers and how much better it is to give than to receive and how if you want to get into the kingdom of heaven then you'd be well advised to sell up and give the proceeds away, because it's easier for a camel to get through the eye of a needle than for a rich man to get into the kingdom . . .

I have read somewhere that we are not to take the needle analogy seriously—that, in fact, Jesus was referring to a particular gate through which a camel could pass with a bit of a squeeze.

Nonsense! He meant a needle, as in a pointy thing with thread. And if he didn't then he should have—it makes the point (a divine pun!) much better. What's more, Jesus said that you should not kill your enemies. In fact, you should surprise them by doing good to them because in the end the person who lives by the sword will die the same way. Furthermore, he told his followers that they shouldn't even hate their enemies, which is a very radical idea indeed.

Jesus reckoned that every man he met was his brother just as much as his blood siblings were and every woman was his mother, just as much as the woman who bore him. He had some very good advice about not spending too much time and effort in filling your barns because who knows, tomorrow you could be dead. Don't even think about tomorrow, he said, today is enough to be getting on with.

You just ended a sentence with two prepositions!

I'm God. I can do that sort of thing.

So there was no virgin birth?

Look, belief, as George Bernard Shaw once said, is a matter of taste. I would have thought that in this day and age the taste for virgin births would not be widespread.

What about the resurrection?

Same thing. Do you believe that people can come back from the dead? I mean, Jesus was supposed to have been really dead. This is not some sort of resuscitation from a coma we are talking about here. Do you believe that sort of thing can happen?

Well, the theory is that You can do anything You want. If You feel like raising someone from the dead then, presto, no sooner thought than done.

Let me tell you again—and no doubt I will have to say it over and over—I do not 'do' things. I am not a human analogue. I do not say: 'Well, here's an idea. Let's have a resurrection.' And then somehow I stir the dirt with My finger and behold, one formerly dead person walking around as large as life. I do not go through the human process of thought, intention and action. How can I make this plainer to you?

I have already told you that I am only in the business of setting up possibilities. In this universe a certain number of things are possible, and therefore at some place they will happen, even if they are as improbable as the emergence of life from inorganic particles.

So now we must look at the question in this way: in a universe of a finite number of possibilities is recovery from death one of them? Have you ever seen it happen? Has it ever been reliably reported to you in a form you found credible?

But Jesus is supposed to have been a special divine/ human being to whom the normal rules of physics don't apply.

Well, that's a matter of belief again—which is a matter of taste. You don't need any word from Me on the subject. You will believe it if you want to or disbelieve if that is more to your taste. The proposition that Jesus was a 'divine/human being' is not really open to proof or refutation is it? I just ask you to consider this. Given what you know about the universe and about the behaviour of matter and the fragility of life and the irreversibility of death, do you think it is likely that two or three people in history have come back from the dead? I say two or three because the Jesus story includes Lazarus and the daughter of Jairus being brought back from the dead. If you want one then you have to take all three— and why stop there?

There is an excellent resurrection story involving Saint Nicholas. It is reliably reported that Saint Nicholas restored to life three little boys who during a famine had been pickled in brine by an unscrupulous butcher. Intending to pass them off as pork, I should imagine. Nicholas arrived at lunchtime and was just about to tuck into a pickled boy when he reeled back, passed a miracle and before you could say abracadabra the boys were up and running around and their mums were pleased as punch.

Do you believe that?

Well, no . . .

Why not? There were eyewitnesses. And if I want to
perform a miracle through the good Nicholas, the
prototype for Father Christmas, who says I can't do it?
After all, am I not the creator of the universe?

Yes, You are . . .

So who's to say I can't do something as simple as unpickle
three boys? Come now. Where's your faith? What do
we have here? A hierarchy of belief? Jesus rises from
the dead—yes, we can believe that. Lazarus? Probably?
The Jairus child? Possibly? The pickled boys, Timothy,
Mark and John? No, that doesn't sound likely. Why not?
After all, your argument for belief is based on the
assertion that the Creator of the Universe can do whatever
She wants to do.

And My response to that is that I don't *do* anything!

*But Jesus called himself the son of God—and if that
is not true then he was a braggart and a liar and that
then discredits everything he said.*

Codswallop. Look, the gospels are not history. They are
religious books written in a prescientific age when people
believed all sorts of things. They were written by men
who were deluded about the extent of My interest in
what goes on on this minor planet in this insignificant
solar system. They thought that they were at the centre
of everything and that the sun went up and down every
day entirely for their benefit. Such people are bound
to believe and say lots of foolish things. They were
superstitious. They were overzealous PR people for a
new religion, a hard enterprise to get off the ground
at the best of times.

What's more, they were frightened of just about
everything. Imagine a world without painless dentistry
and devoid of so much as an aspirin. Life was no bed
of roses, I can tell you. How do you explain lightning

if you know nothing about electricity? Easy—you call it god. How do people who know nothing about bacteria and viruses explain disease? Easy—call it the devil. Mental illness is called demonic possession. Every inexplicable natural phenomenon is a sign of God's pleasure or displeasure. It is a primitive, childish cosmology and in that particular world view miraculous births and resurrections and miraculous beings were to be expected. Ask yourself, with absolute honesty, if someone came knocking on your door today and said: 'Good afternoon, I am the son of God. Follow me, please,'—what would you say or do?

Belief, you know, is not only a matter of taste. It is also a matter of prejudice. Or perhaps that's what Shaw meant, anyway.

Take the case of Joseph Smith, the original Mormon. He claims that he was led by an angel to a spot where the Book of Mormon, inscribed on gold plates, was buried. He dug it up and found that it was written in 'reformed Egyptian'. Never mind. It seems that I furnished him with a pair of magic spectacles called *Urim* and *Thummim*. Using these Smith was able to translate the story. Unhappily, when some sceptics asked to see the golden tablets and the magic specs he had to report that the angels had taken it all away again.

Millions of people believe that story. Do you?

Well, no . . .

Why not? Are you calling the founder of the Church of Jesus Christ of the Latterday Saints and all his followers liars and charlatans?

Dear me, that's a hard question to deal with . . .

Why?

Well, good manners tells us that we shouldn't scoff at other people's religions. I mean, there are people who believe that all sorts of things in this country were made

*by giant serpents or dingoes or kangaroos or whatever
and we are supposed to treat this very seriously. In fact
we have laws in this country which prohibit scoffing
at anyone's religious beliefs, no matter how stupid.*

Really? What a very novel idea. Do you mean to say—
just to think up an interesting hypothesis—that if a
person were to write a book giving offence to some
religious group and that that religious group were to
proclaim the death sentence on the said author that you
would not be permitted to ridicule the aforementioned
religious group?

Well, yes—I think that's the way it works.

How very curious. I'm all for tolerance, but I think you
should be warned that when the tolerant is confronted
with intolerance ridicule could well be your best weapon.
    Anyway, I am not asking you to scoff at anything.
Keep a perfectly straight face. Think kind and courteous
thoughts. Wish all true believers everywhere great happiness and contentment. Promise never to persecute them
or to make them miserable. Be most wise, tolerant, kind
and liberal. But now, tell me honestly, do you believe
in the golden plates and the magical spectacles.

Since You put it that way, no . . .

Do you believe in creative serpents?

No.

Do you believe in astrology, tarot cards, palm reading,
crystal-ball gazing or water divining?

*Well, I'm not sure about water divining—but on the
other things, no.*

Why not? If you have an anthropomorphic notion of
God as a human analogue, but with limitless powers,
sitting just above the sky, then anything is possible.
    I have heard people say this. If God is the all-powerful

Creator of the universe, then She can do anything She wants to. But they overlook the limit of the ridiculous.

Consider this. Here I am—almighty! Omnipotent! Omniscient! And so on. There is nothing, absolutely nothing, that I cannot do. Agreed?

Well, yes, I suppose so . . .

Right! Standby! I am about to make a caterpillar drive a double-decker bus up a spiral staircase. Are you ready?

Oh come on—don't be ridiculous . . .

Ah hah! My point precisely! *Don't be ridiculous!* That is the limit to what is possible in this system in which you live. It is the limit of the ridiculous. The more credulous will draw the line limiting the ridiculous at some point between the resurrection of Jesus and the resurrection of the pickled boys. The more sceptical and rational will draw a very sharp and precise line between what she knows from observation is possible and what in fact happens from time to time and that which she has never observed and of which she has never had a reliable, eyewitness account. So for the rationalist the limit of the ridiculous will be drawn on the sceptical side of virgin birth, water walking and resurrection. Never mind magic spectacles, tablets of gold, angels, serpents, tarot cards and the zodiac. If a thing is self-evidently ridiculous then you are not obliged to waste any time or mental energy in demonstrating that it is untrue. It is axiomatic.

If this were not so then the universe would be such an unpredictable and whimsical system that you would hardly dare leave home in the morning. But you do go about your daily routine precisely because you know that effects must always have an adequate cause. In other words, everything that happens has an explanation in physics—and that which cannot be subject to the analysis of physics is not worth thinking about, except as titillating fantasy.

But what about love and beauty and art and music—these are all supposed to be mysteries which are beyond scientific accountability.

That is nonsense. 'Love' is the urge to procreate and to protect the offspring. Music and art have physical explanations. 'Beauty' is partly a physical response to aural or visual stimuli and partly a socially conditioned preference for some forms over others. You may describe the perfume of lavender as divine and the aroma of manure as rank—but to a blowfly the exact opposite may be true.

Gosh, You certainly know how to take the magic out of life's occasional sublime experiences.

Rubbish. If I took a Mozart aria apart note by note and gave you a scientific explanation for why this combination of frequencies, intervals and modulations sounds harmonious to you that would not destroy the pleasure of the whole, would it? If I showed you how Rembrandt unconsciously used the physics of light to achieve his effects it would not diminish the pleasure you take from a Rembrandt painting in its entirety.

Are You sure that it's not possible to know too much for our own good?

Never! That is existential cowardice. Face facts. Miracles are intellectually preposterous. Give them up. They are bad for you.

You don't need any miraculous elements for a truly instructive and inspiring Jesus story. Here is a Jesus story which is so profound that the canon of scripture should be re-opened to find a spot for it. It is called *The Dancing Fool*, and this is how it goes:

A flying saucer creature named Zog arrived on earth to explain how wars could be prevented, and how cancer could be cured. Zog brought the information from Margo, a planet where the natives conversed by means of farts and tap-dancing. Zog landed at night in Connecticut. He had no sooner touched down than he saw a house on fire. He rushed into the house, farting and tap-dancing, warning people about the terrible danger they were in. The head of the house brained him with a golf club.[1]

Which is more or less the Jesus story in a nutshell.

Or here's another version of the same idea. This one comes from the Danish theologian Sören Kierkegaard. It is in his book *Either/Or*.

What happens to those who try to warn the present age?

It happened that a fire broke out backstage in a theatre. The clown came out to inform the public. They thought it was just a jest and applauded. He repeated his warning, then shouted even louder. So I think the world will come to an end amid general applause from all the wits, who believe that it is a joke.

May we talk about Christianity as an institutional phenomenon?

It is painful for Me, but why not?

---

[1] This splendid Jesus story comes from Kurt Vonnegut's book *Fates Worse than Death* (Jonathon Cape, London, 1991, p 209). He says it is the outline for a short story which he has never written. But what more can there possibly be to say? Is this not a masterpiece just as it is?

· 4 ·

Religion

So, may we talk about religion?

Yes, if you must—although I warn you that it is a subject about which I have little patience, because it usually involves blaming Me for things that I have never done.

Really, what in particular?

Oh, making someone's enemy into a footstool or smiting him hip and thigh or laying waste to this, that or the other.

Or there is the other wimpy stuff about thanking Me

for saving someone from a catastrophe in which I have not the slightest interest.

It really is a peculiar delusion that religious people have that, somehow, what happens to an individual member of the species *Homo sapiens* is of sufficient interest for Me to actually *do* something about. I mean, how many humans are there on the earth at the moment? Five billion, give or take a few? And there are billions of other life forms, all of interest, in a cosmic sense— and on top of that there are another six planets with interesting life forms—and yet some individual members of the human species are vain enough to think that I would somehow activate a bit of Myself to intervene on their behalf to frustrate some natural sequence of cause and effect. Does that not strike you as presumptuous?

However, before we talk about that, let's talk about religion. Any particular one? There are plenty from which to choose.

Well, Christianity is the one I know best—can we talk about that?

All right, but let's start with a few general observations about religion so that we can agree on what it is we are discussing.

I assume that the first religious impulse comes from the need to find an explanation for natural phenomena. When humans acquired speech I imagine that the first thing they said to each other was: 'Where has all this come from?' And the only logical answer, for a pre-scientific human, must have been: 'Someone, like us only bigger, must have made it all.'

In which case, this bigger being who stands somewhere else and makes all these things, must also somehow be responsible for all the mischief done by fire, flood, drought and disease. We had best do something to make Him or Her well disposed towards us. We'll sacrifice a goat. No, hang on, how about a virgin? Or the heart of an enemy? And so came the idea that somehow the

Almighty's pleasure was sacrifice of some sort, the gorier and more gruesome it was the more efficacious it was thought to be.

Then in no time there was a class of persons designated for making sacrifices and for addressing praises and requests to the Almighty—and lo, you have a religion with priests in fancy dress and temples and all the other paraphernalia of religion. Followed immediately by the discovery that other tribes have different religions, which cannot be tolerated, under any circumstances. Your God, it goes without saying, is a jealous God and if there's one thing He can't stand it's competition. Thus began the wars of religion, for which I tend to get all the blame.

It so happens that one part of the religious phenomenon is understandable. Given the sheer mysteriousness of the universe and life itself, and given that it appeals both to the aesthetic and curiosity faculties of humans, why shouldn't you try to express your surprise and admiration in words and rituals? Perfectly understandable. But all this other stuff is simply superstition.

Now Jesus, if I understand him correctly—and if I don't, who does?—was of a mind to do away with religion altogether in its formal, institutionalised sense. He was all for a Kingdom of God that was within. You would have to say that he was a spiritual anarchist who reckoned that the individual could get along quite well without the benefit of an organisation. In fact, it was his spiritual anarchy that got him into trouble with the men who ran the religious institution of his time. All this talk about destroying temples and calling the religious bureaucrats 'whitened sepulchres' was bound to do him no good in the end.

Which brings us to one of the most curious consequences of the Jesus event. The very man who was executed for failing to pay proper respect to the religious bureaucracy of his time came to be associated with the biggest, most quarrelsome, cruel, superstitious religious institutions the world has ever seen.

You don't believe me? Consider this. Within a couple of hundred years the followers of Jesus—who were still an outlawed, heretical minority at the time—were arguing about *homo-ousion* and *homo-iousion*. I've already mentioned this argument. Do you know what that means?

Well, if I've got it the right way around, the *homo-ousionists* reckoned that Jesus and I were the same and the *homo-iousionists* were adamant that we were only a lot like each other. Can you imagine? This nonsense, which hinged on a single iota, was the main preoccupation of the Jesusites for hundreds of years. But, of course, things got worse. I've lost count of the number of people who have been burned, garrotted, disembowelled, beheaded, drowned and simply slaughtered by one lot of Christians trying to change the minds of other Christians on important subjects like this.

Consider the Thirty Years War. This was Catholic against Protestant Jesusites. They were warring over the jurisdiction of the Bishop of Rome. And it happened mainly in Germany between 1618 and 1648. In 1618 there were sixteen million people in Germany. In 1648 there were six million.[1] Can you imagine that? And all done to defend the reputation and honour of Jesus, the prince of peace, who once said that the peacemakers would be really happy because they would get a special recognition from Me. Amazing, is it not?

Do you know why the Black Death took such a terrible toll in Europe in the fourteenth century? Because the Jesusites had this amazing notion that there were witches everywhere and that cats were their familiars— so it wasn't enough to burn the witches (thousands of them, incidentally), they had to also stamp out the cats. So there were no cats to kill the rats, which bred

---

[1] Williston Walker, *A History of the Christian Church*, T & T Clark, Edinburgh, 1957, p 451

like rodents and carried the infected fleas all over the place.[2]

The witch-hunts, which lasted for hundreds of years, showed what terrible crimes can be committed when superstition rules the actions of bishops and popes. Just to give you a couple of examples. In 1678 the Archbishop of Salzburg had seventy-nine women burned because their witchcraft was causing the deaths of cattle around about the town. In 1630 or thereabouts the Bishop of Bamberg had about 900 witches and sorcerers executed. The Bishop of Würtzburg despatched about 1200 witches via the stake. And the Archbishop of Treves was so enthusiastic about hunting down and murdering women who had had intercourse with the Devil that by 1585 two villages in his diocese could only count four women altogether in their populations.[3]

The youngest witch burned for sorcery, at least as far as the records show, was four years old. There was no upper age limit.

The method of examining suspected witches is interesting. First the woman was asked if she believed in witches. If she said no, then she was by definition a witch and in league with the Prince of Liars. On the other hand, if she said yes, she was immediately asked where she was on Thursday night when the storm broke or the cows died.

She would then be examined for physical signs that she had been with the Devil. She would be stripped and shaved and any mole, wart or birthmark would be enough to seal her fate. John Calvin, the great Genevan reformer, and beyond all doubt a great Christian,

[2] *The Lancet*, 22 August 1987, p 450 (in a letter from T S Szasz, University Hospital, Syracuse NY)
[3] Joachim Kahl, in his book *The Misery of Christianity* (Melbourne, 1972), Pelican, catalogues the atrocities committed in the name of Christ over the centuries. Kahl reckons that a study of church history is a sure recipe for atheism. He also deals with the 'children of their times' and 'not true christians' arguments.

advocated mass executions to make sure that the witches didn't get away.

Just as a matter of historical interest, the last witches were burnt in Switzerland in 1782 and the last ones drowned near Danzig in 1836.[4] Not so long ago, is it?

And the worst of all this is that I am held responsible for it all. I am supposed to have said to Moses: 'You shall not permit a sorceress to live.'[5] Can you imagine Me saying that?

Mind you, while knowing nothing about fleas and germs some Jesusites thought that they had hit on a cure for the plague. Kill the Jews! The Jews were supposed to have carried the plague poison from Toledo in their little black bags, and to have sprinkled it into wells and springs.

In fact, many Jews admitted as much. Not at first, but after they had had the question put to them in the torture chambers of the Inquisition they overcame their natural reluctance to confess.

In Savoy in 1348 eleven Jews were burned alive and the rest were taxed at 160 florins every month for six years. Which set off a wave of torture and killings throughout Europe until intervention came from an unlikely source. Pope Clement VI sent a letter around to the Churches saying that anyone who believed the Jews were spreading the plague had been seduced by 'that liar, the Devil'. Which was fair enough, except that he didn't leave it there. He told his underlings that the plague came about because of a 'mysterious decree of God'. Me!

But at least Clement showed a bit of sense and logic. Seeing that Jews were as susceptible to the buboes as Christians it was hard to believe that they were deliberately causing their own misery just to spite the

4 *ibid*, pp 83–5
5 Exodus 22:18

Christians. But that outbreak of commonsense didn't do an awful lot of good. Five months later in Basle the entire Jewish community of several hundred people was herded into a specially constructed wooden house on an island in the Rhine and the good Christians of Basle set fire to it. And just to make sure that that was that, the town passed a decree banning Jews from the place for the next 200 years.

Meanwhile, in Strasbourg the 2000 Jews in the town were taken to the cemetery and given a humane choice: convert to Christianity or be burned at the stake. At Worms and Frankfurt-am-Main the Jews took matters into their own hands and committed mass suicide by setting fire to their homes and burning themselves before the Christians arrived.[6]

Will I tell you about the Anabaptists? Harmless enough heretics, you would have thought. They thought that baptism of babies was defective—that you should only be baptised after you had made up your own mind to become a Christian. And then it should be done by total immersion. The great Protestant reformer, Huldreich Zwingli, running the town of Zurich in 1526, approved of the particular punishment decreed for the Anabaptists—they were drowned in the lake in parody of their peculiar ritual![7] And it's such a pretty lake. Have you ever been there?

An ironic consequence of this persecution of the Anabaptists is that they became famous and popular and for a time rivalled the Lutherans in their growth rate. Can you explain that? Funny people, these Christians.

Do you know about the St Bartholomew's Day massacre in France? 8000 Huguenots murdered in Paris alone—no one kept count of the dead outside the capital.

---

[6] Barbara Tuchman, *A Distant Mirror*, Macmillan, London, 1978, pp 112–3
[7] Walker, p 367

They say that the Seine ran red for days.[8] Such a pretty river, too.

I could go on like this for days—Christians killing Christians; Christians killing Jews; Jews killing Muslims; Muslims killing Jews and Christians and so on— and to make matters worse, every one of the murderers claims that I told him to do it.

Where do they get such an idea?

But these men who persecuted witches and Jews and other Christians were children of their times, surely . . .

What on earth does that mean?

Well, they were only acting like everyone else at the time. No one knew any better.

Well, I must say that that is several kinds of self-deluding nonsense.

To start with, if it were ever true that there was a time when absolutely no one 'knew any better' then you would still have trial by ordeal, slavery, child labour and witch-hunts. There have always been people who 'knew better'. They have been the heretics, the dissenters, the radicals and the troublemakers. From time to time— going back to the earliest years of the Church—there have even been popes who have railed against anti-Semitism.

The Gnostics in Alexandria in the second century abolished slavery and accorded equal rights to women because they believed in the equality of all humanity. Why didn't their ideas catch on instead of the idea that persisted for centuries that some humans were inferior? Indeed, in the case of women it was the argument of Thomas Aquinas that was held to be the last word on the matter. He proved from scripture and philosophy that women were not really human—just some sort of

---

[8] *ibid*, p 435

defective parody of men through whom sin entered the
world.

While the Crusaders were wading up to their ankles
in blood in Jerusalem there were priests like Francis of
Assisi and Anselm of Canterbury preaching peace and
condemning the Crusades. Why weren't they listened to,
rather than Pope Urban II who presumed, on My behalf,
to offer forgiveness of sins to everyone who took part
and a guarantee of eternal life if they should have the
misfortune to be killed?

Incidentally, once the first Crusading army was assem-
bled and marching towards the Holy Land they got in
some practice on the way. 'Many Jews were massacred
in the Rhine cities.'[9] It makes you wonder what counted
as a 'sin' needing forgiveness, doesn't it.

Richard the Lionheart—remember him? the good
friend of Robin Hood—had 2000 to 3000 Muslim captives
murdered during the Third Crusade and then had their
entrails examined for captured gold. Waste not, want
not, I suppose. But the one thing that you cannot claim
in vindication of Richard is that he was a 'child of his
times' and that 'no one knew any better'. Many people
knew better. Their message fell on wilfully deaf ears.

The Waldenses objected to the Inquisition and to all
forms of trial by torture and indeed, to all forms of
shedding blood. You won't be surprised to hear that they
were excommunicated—and because they had got their
pernicious ideas from the Bible a law was passed at the
synod of Toulouse in 1229 forbidding ordinary Christians to read the Bible because it could lead to all sorts
of folly.

Zwingli had no problems dealing with the Anabaptists
by drowning them precisely because they *did know better*.
They were radical pacifists and wouldn't fight back.

Look, I could go on and on—there never was a time

---

[9] *ibid*, p 240

when there wasn't someone who knew better and was prepared to stick his or her neck out. The tragedy was that they tended to get short shrift in the Church. Given the choice between light and darkness, the Church could usually be counted on to choose darkness.

If I could interrupt here, there are a lot of people who say that You talk to them and tell them to do things. It's called 'revelation'. You are supposed to have revealed all sorts of things about how You want humans to behave and what You want us to believe. I mean, what about the Ten Commandments? Didn't You give them to Moses? And the burning bush? Wasn't that You?

You don't really believe that, do you? What would I *reveal*? What is there to reveal?

Well, I presume that You would reveal what You want . . .

Want? I don't *want* anything. You really are suffering from a chronic case of anthropomorphisms. If I wanted something then I suppose—and this is purely hypothetical, you understand—it would just happen. How can God want something without there being an immediate puff of smoke and it coming to pass, as it were.

I don't want anything in particular. As far as I am concerned it all just happens. I am indifferent. Disinterested. I've told you before, I just deal in possibilities.

To take the case of Moses and the conversation I am supposed to have had with him. Who needs ten commandments? Commonsense tells you that every choice you make involves at least two possible outcomes. You could end up making other people happier or miserable. That's all there is to it. And any attempt to confuse the issue with concepts like good and evil will only make matters infinitely worse, because these are grand and terrible delusions. We might talk about them later.

What's more, it was in that very same conversation that I am supposed to have had with Moses that I am reported to have said: 'You shall not suffer a sorceress to live.' And 'Whoever lies with a beast shall be put to death.' And 'Whoever sacrifices to any God, save to the Lord (that's Me!) shall be utterly destroyed.' And— I like this one—'You shall not boil a kid in its mother's milk.'[10] I am actually reported to have said that more than once, so it must be very important. Unfortunately, I have forgotten what the penalty is for boiling a kid in its mother's milk, but I imagine that it involves eternal torment of some kind.

You're making a joke of all this.

Well, what else can I make of it? But you see the problem that it poses for you, don't you? You can't possibly believe that I actually said all this nonsense to Moses—but in amongst all of this I am supposed to have dictated the Ten Commandments, and you want to hold onto them as a piece of authentic divine conversation. Well, you can't. You have to take it all, or none at all.

Look, here in Deuteronomy it says that I have decreed that 'He whose testicles are crushed or whose male member is cut off shall not enter the assembly of the Lord. No bastard shall enter the assembly of the Lord; even to the tenth generation none of his descendants shall enter the assembly of the Lord.'[11] That means you, I believe. The bastard bit, I mean.

That is very unkind.

Exactly. And do you think that I would be so unkind? Do you really, seriously, believe that I would have said any of this? Of course not. So you have to face the fact that you can't pick and choose. If I didn't say the stuff about the testicles then I didn't dictate the commandments. Moses—or someone—made them up. By and large

[10] Exodus 22:18ff
[11] Deuteronomy 23:1-2

they seem to be reasonable rules for prudent communal living. Let's leave it at that and not try to claim some special divine authority for them, shall we?

So even though over the centuries there have been many people who have claimed that You have spoken to them personally, You have never actually said anything to anyone? Apart from this conversation, of course . . .

Never. Don't you think that if I had said something to someone that that would be the last word on everything?

And supposing I did, right now, give you the very last word—as I am supposed to have done to Moses, Elijah and Joan of Arc. Who would believe you when you told them? If they didn't particularly care for the message, whatever it was, they would call you a crackpot, wouldn't they?

I mean, let's suppose the message was: 'Stop eating meat! Eating meat is the root of all evil. I have made all you creatures to live together on the planet and eat grass, and look what you have done. You've turned the place into a slaughterhouse. It has to stop.'

Now you put on sackcloth and ashes and walk up and down the country crying: 'Stop eating meat! God has told me to tell you that She only loves vegetarians. Believe me, this is straight from the lips of the Almighty Herself.'

There are people who believe that eating meat is a biological crime—and they would greet you as the new vegetarian Messiah and make a terrific fuss over you. The cattle farmers, on the other hand, would say that you are a crackpot and have you crucified, figuratively, at least. So what's the point in Me telling anyone any-thing? Until you have worked it out for yourselves and arrived at some sort of consensus on the matter anything that I have to say will have no more power to convince than a pronouncement on the same subject by a politician or a priest.

So You never talk to anyone?

Never.

What about Bob Haifley of Cavina in California?

Who?

Bob Haifley. He swears that one day he was sitting in his truck when You said to him: 'Bob, I want you to build a life-size figure of Jesus using toothpicks.'

I said that?

It was in the papers.[12] It says that Bob said to You: 'Gee, I can't do that. You're asking me to undertake a task that will take ten years.'

How did he work that out on the spot? I'm not sure that I could have calculated the time needed to make a toothpick Jesus that quickly.

Well, anyway, Bob got a pair of tweezers, some glue and 65 000 toothpicks—some round, some flat, some square—and 2500 hours later he had the job finished. And You told him to call it The Gift.

I did? Where is it now?

It says here that it is hanging on wires in Bob's garage.

There you are then. Do I need to say any more?

What about the Emperor Constantine who saw a flaming cross in the sky and heard You say: 'In this sign, conquer'?

Then what happened?

Well, it was at the battle of Mulvian Bridge near Rome in 312, and he won. It is regarded as a turning point for Christianity.

---

[12] *Sunday Age*, Melbourne, 1 September 1991

And how many people were killed as a result of this peculiar revelation?

I don't know—quite a few, I suppose.

Do you think that I give special orders for killing 'quite a few' people?

You must have done. The Bible is absolutely full of stories of You telling people to kill Canaanites or Amalekites or whomever. It says here in I Samuel: 'Thus says the Lord of hosts, ". . . Now go and smite Amalek and utterly destroy all that they have; do not spare them, but kill both man and woman, infant and suckling, ox and sheep, camel and ass." '[13] And Saul got into terrible trouble for not carrying out Your orders to the letter. Samuel said to him: '. . . the Lord God sent you on a mission, and said, "Go, utterly destroy the sinners, the Amalekites, and fight against them until they are consumed." Why then did you not obey the voice of the Lord?'[14] It's here in the Bible, so it must be true.

Would you give such an order?

No, of course not. It's terrible. It's what we would call an atrocity these days.

But you think that I don't mind about atrocities?

Well, Your ways are mysterious and ineffable and beyond knowing, so I'm told.

That may be so. But morality is morality. And a thing cannot be moral in a religious sense and immoral in a secular sense, can it? Truth is one. That which is true scientifically cannot be untrue religiously, can it? If it is scientifically true that the earth revolves around the sun and not the sun around the earth, then that is the

---

[13] 1 Samuel 15:3
[14] 1 Samuel 15:18–19

truth of the matter and religion must be made to fit what we know empirically to be true.

And that's the way it is with morality. An act cannot be evil in a secular sense and good in a religious sense. So if what Saul did to the Amalekites was the sort of thing that these days would attract the attention of Amnesty how can it be good in some sort of divine moral scheme of things? Can you explain that to Me?

It is as silly as thinking that I would tell anyone to make a toothpick Jesus. What sort of God am I if I am a constant affront to commonsense and morality?

I can't answer that. But there are so many things that are hard to understand. There are many true believers who are convinced that there is nothing that happens that You don't either will or permit. You've already mentioned that people say things like: 'God permits famines and floods to test the compassion of Christians.'

Do you mean to say that I would deliberately connive at human suffering in some miserable, backward, drought-prone country in order to check out the generosity of those who live in more abundant climes? Are you suggesting that I would arrange things so that millions of people could starve to death as part of a sort of experiment to test whether or not you are as generous as you ought to be?

It has been put forward as an explanation of why You, the omnipotent God who can do everything, should apparently turn a blind eye to suffering on this magnitude.

I don't have an 'eye'. In fact I don't 'see' anything. I do wish that you would grow out of this anthropomorphic image that you have of Me.

Anyway, on the subject of saying things to people— I doubt that it would make much difference if I said anything to anyone about anything. Jesusites claim to be impressed and influenced by what Jesus had to say.

In fact, most would reckon that anything Jesus had to say was really coming from Me in the first place.

Which makes it all the more staggering, from a purely human point of view you understand, because God cannot be staggered, that Jesusites manage to totally ignore the simple, straightforward and unambiguous things that Jesus said while at the same time being utterly dogmatic about the vague, peripheral and ambiguous parts of the story.

Let's take the baptism example again. Here is Zwingli, a famously pious and wise man, goes to Church every Sunday, reckons that he knows more than the Pope and has a very special, personal insight into what Jesus had to say on all manner of subjects, and he's so adamant about baptism that he can be quite sanguine about the drowning of the Anabaptists. Now this, you must admit, is peculiar behaviour. Zwingli never had anything definite to say on the subject of war, except that it was a perfectly acceptable means of settling religious arguments, and yet he cared so deeply about baptism.

Now it so happens that the gospels are very light on when it comes to advice about the proper age and mode of baptism. You can make out a case either way. And in the end it doesn't seem to matter so much that you would actually consider drowning those whose interpretation differs from your own.

On the other hand, Jesus said quite a lot about war and violence. There is no doubt that by teaching and example Jesus was a pacifist. His death was by a particularly cruel form of execution—and if you thought that the Communists were on their way to your country to do that sort of thing to you you would probably think: We'd better kill them before they get here to do that to us. Very reasonable in the circumstances. But you know what Jesus said? 'Forgive them, because they don't know what they are doing.' In other words, there can be absolutely no doubt what Jesus thought of war and murder and violence in general. Yet there have been precious few religious bureaucrats who have ever said anything unequivocal on the subject of war, but on baptism you can't shut them up.

Or take this business of women becoming priests. There is absolutely nothing in the gospels which would settle the matter one way or the other. Jesus clearly didn't think that it was worth saying anything on a subject about which you ought to be able to take a non-discriminatory consensus for granted. And yet here we have big Christian corporations of the Anglican, Orthodox and Catholic stripe keeping women out of the top jobs on the basis of biblical evidence that doesn't exist.

And all the time the gospels make it perfectly plain that a basic part of Jesus's prescription for the ideal society is voluntary socialism and a sort of cheerful austerity. He worried away incessantly at the issue of the poor and the inequitable distribution of wealth. He was fixated on it. Well, I suppose that some timid things are being said by the Christians on this subject at long last. But it's taken a long time to see the obvious. Very perverse, if you ask Me, to be fussed about ordination, baptism, trinities, transubstantiation and consubstantiation—none of which gets an unambiguous definition in the gospels—while turning a blind eye to the obvious, that Jesus was all for peaceful and joyful austerity and a mutual responsibility for each other's happiness and well-being.

But you see what I mean? Religions get hung up on the esoteric trivia and ignore the simple and essential parts of Jesus's prescription for a kingdom of God on earth. Or as Jesus said—and very well, if you ask Me— they strain at a gnat and swallow the camel.

There is one other thing that I would like to talk about before we get away from the subject of religion, and that is the business of Church services themselves. They are supposed to be for Your benefit, I suppose. You are supposed to be terrifically impressed with our loyalty and our hymn singing and praying and so on. Does it matter?

Well, of course it doesn't matter to Me—but does it matter to you? I certainly hope that you're not putting yourself to all this trouble on My behalf. How can you expect to impress Me? You're not suggesting that these weekly rituals are My idea, are you?

Well, there is a general belief around to that effect.

In that case let Me put the record straight. What you do in church is for your benefit, not mine. If you like getting together with your friends for a bit of a singsong and some mutual cheering up and a few life-improving rituals every week then I think that that is very nice . . .

Nice?

What else can I say? Let me tell you a joke I heard the other day. We are in New York. There is a squeal of brakes and a thud. A man has been hit by a car. A little Jewish lady comes rushing out of her apartment block with a saucepan and a spoon. She pushes her way through the crowd of stickybeaks and starts to ladle chicken soup into the mouth of the injured man. Someone says: 'Chicken soup? How can that help?' And the old lady says: 'It might not help, but it coitanly can't hoit!' Which is more or less all that I have to say on the subject of church services. Except for one other thing.

A scientist—an astronomer, in fact—who goes to church every Sunday (to one of the ones that reckons that women are not fit to have the best jobs) said once: 'The act of worship may have very little to do with the mind, nevertheless the mind must not be offended. The only refuge for the critical mind is to disengage itself from what is being said . . .'[15]

---

[15] Professor Robert Hanbury Brown says that in his book *The Wisdom of Science* (CUP, Cambridge, 1986, p 165).

Now, how can you do that? You would have to have your brain in neutral for just about the whole of the service. You couldn't say: 'Our Father, who art in Heaven . . .' Father is offensive to more than half the congregation, and in any case I resent being lumbered with a title which implies that somehow or other I am involved in sexual reproduction. And where, pray, is heaven? And who says that I am responsible for your daily bread?

Or take the creeds. What are you going to do with your brain while you are reciting this?

> We believe in one God, the Father Almighty, maker of all things, both visible and invisible; and in one Lord, Jesus Christ, the Son of God, only begotten of the Father, that is to say, of the substance of the Father, God of God and Light of Light, very God of very God, begotten, not made, being of one substance with the Father by whom all things were made, both things in heaven and things on earth; who, for us men and for our salvation, came down and was made flesh, was made man, suffered, and rose again on the third day, went up into the heavens and is to come again to judge both the quick and the dead; and in the Holy Ghost.

This curious formula is known as the Nicene Creed and was cobbled together at the Council of Nicaea in 325. The emperor, Constantine, was there, beginning an alliance of Church and state which has caused more misery than all the plagues, famines and droughts of history put together. You won't be surprised to hear that the two delegates to the conference who refused to sign this nonsense were banished by the emperor—who, by the way, was not even a Christian at that stage.

Now this creed, you must admit, lays it on a bit thick. The 'very God of very God' seems a trifle redundant after 'God of God', and then to add the 'being of one substance' line smacks of overkill. That is *homo-ousion*, incidentally. The truly amazing thing is that a bunch

of grown men could have frittered away their time con-
cocting this farrago of superstition. This is what happens
when an ignorant, prescientific cosmology is mated with
the linguistic sophistication of Greece and Rome. But
for all that it is meaningless.

One unsympathetic observer at Nicaea wrote that the
majority of the participants were 'simpletons'. You
probably didn't need to be told.[16]

If I were running the Church I would—as a matter
of some urgency—reconvene the Council of Nicaea and
draft a new statement of belief that fits the contemporary
knowledge of the universe. Just for a start you would
have to eliminate '. . . went up into the heavens and is
to come again', presumably *down* from the heavens.

Then again, perhaps it's not worth the effort.

What about prayers? Do they do any good?

For whom?

*Well, what I mean is, do You ever actually do what
people ask You to do when they pray?*

Let Me tell you that this is a very touchy subject for Me.
People who pray must have a very peculiar idea of Me.
First, they must assume that I am interested in what some
individual member of the species *Homo sapiens* wants.
And I have already told you that I am not.

Secondly, they assume that I am not paying attention
and need to be reminded of what is going on.

Thirdly, there is an assumption in the prayer activity
that if you ask nicely I will do something that I could
easily have done but through laziness, vanity, inattention
or churlishness have chosen not to do.

Let's take a case in point. Here is a whole church
full of people praying that I will cure the cancer of
someone they know. Now, being a good God, if I could

---

[16] Walker, p 116

have cured her cancer would I not already have done so? Am I so distracted that I haven't noticed? Am I so vain that I want to see a bit of grovelling before I will stir myself to pass a miracle? What on earth do you people think is going on?

Some people even get together to send me climatic prayers. 'Make it rain,' they pray. Or 'make it stop raining', as the case may be. Let's just imagine for a moment that I did make it stop raining or, on the other hand, start raining, over the particular area which the supplicants are drawing to My attention. What will be the consequences elsewhere? If I fiddle with the climate over one part of the globe then we can take it for granted that the effects would be felt all over the place. I mean to say, if the Chaos theory people are right and the flap of a butterfly wing in the Amazon forest can set off climatic changes thousands of kilometres away, just imagine what would happen if I intervened to make it rain or stop raining over Kingaroy. So, just to be on the safe side, the best course of action for me would be to calculate the ideal mix of rain and sunshine for every part of the earth and just fix the whole unpredictable mess up, once and for all, so that from now on everybody gets just the right amount of rain, all of which will fall at night so that your holidays at the beach won't be ruined. How about that? Perfect sunny days without interruption and exactly the right amount of rain every night.

It sounds all right to me.

Of course it's all right. It would be perfect. And if I could do it without giving offence to Myself I suppose that I ought to do it. It would be tantamount to cancelling the second law of thermodynamics, but so what?

You see, we are getting into the ridiculous here again. It is utterly ridiculous to suggest that I can alter the weather. It is as mad as the suggestion that I once made the sun stand still.

And consider this. If there were an outbreak of bubonic

plague today, what would you do? Pray? Or start putting out the rat bait? Where would you expect help to come from—heaven or the medical laboratories?

So you spread this furphy about me—that I could help if I wanted to, but just to be on the safe side we'd better start work on a vaccine. What sort of God am I? Unpredictable, whimsical, unreliable but an ever present help when all else fails. Good grief!

But far and away the silliest prayers are those that come My way during wars. I am expected to bless this or that bomb or battleship or whatever instrument of destruction happens to be launched. I am expected to give victory to the righteous on both sides. But silliest of all are the prayers along the lines of 'O God, please give us peace . . .' To which I can only say: 'You got yourself into this thing, now get yourself out of it.'

Just think about what you call the First World War. About nine million people were killed in four years, most of them true believers in Me. None of them wanted to die. Millions of prayers were recited of the 'please save me', 'please save my daddy', 'please help us kill more Germans/British today' variety. What was I supposed to make of that?

Shaw seemed to be one of the few humans making sense during that carnage. He thought it particularly ironic that during the war the stock exchange was closed as a solemn sign of the inappropriateness of making money while millions were being butchered but the churches stayed open! After all, a lot of profit was made during the war. It cost $30 billion in the money of the time just in property losses and damage. Over $200 billion was spent directly on running the war. You would have thought that the stock exchange would have been full of worshippers at the shrine of my adversary, Mammon, and My churches would have been closed. Shaw made himself terribly unpopular by drawing attention to this irony in a piece called *Common Sense about the War*.

In no previous war have we struck that top note of keen irony, the closing of the Stock Exchange and not of the Church. The pagans were more logical: they closed the Temple of Peace when they drew the sword. We turn our Temples of Peace promptly into temples of war, and exhibit our parsons as the most pugnacious characters in the community. I venture to affirm that the sense of scandal given by this is far deeper and more general than the Church thinks, especially among the working classes, who are apt to either take religion seriously or to repudiate it and criticise it closely. When a Bishop at the first shot rallies his flock around the altar of Mars, he may be acting patriotically, necessarily, manfully, rightly; but that does not justify him in pretending that there has been no change and that Christ is, in effect, Mars.

I couldn't have put it better Myself. The idea of stock-brokers having a keener sense of shame than priests appeals to My ineffable sense of humour.

As a matter of fact, Shaw thought that it was You writing his words. He once wrote that he 'only guided the pen of the Life Force as the husbandman guides its plough' and he said that his 'only pride in the matter is to write legibly and tempt the world to read with the cunning that we call the writer's word'.[17]

That's very presumptuous of him! But on the whole I would rather be held responsible for what Shaw wrote than for most of what passes for 'inspired' scripture or theology. If I were to appoint anyone to write on my behalf it would probably be GBS.

---

[17] The Shaw quotes are from *Shaw on Religion*, a compilation of Shaw's writings on the subject edited by Warren Sylvester Smith and published by Constable in 1967. It is the most used, most battered book in my library. Shaw believed in a Life Force or *Elan Vital*, which proceeds by a process of trial and error. When the Life Force makes a mistake it throws up some new creature to eliminate its previous blunders. So humans, according to Shaw, should not take it for granted that they are the Life Force's last evolutionary word. If we don't 'come up to the mark' then the Life Force will dispose of us as matter-of-factly as it disposed of the dinosaurs.

Just to get back to the war for a minute—the tragedy is that most of the nine million or so people who were killed volunteered for the slaughter.

Surely not? Most of the belligerent nations had conscription.

That's true—but the men who were called up didn't have to obey the call-up, did they? They could have simply refused to go. In the end they went meekly off to the slaughterhouse. I find that very hard to understand.

But it says in the Bible that we must obey the civil authority because 'there is no authority except from God, and those that exist have been instituted by God. Therefore he who resists the authorities resist what God has appointed, and those who resist will incur judgement.'[18]

Well, here's a pretty how-de-do. Am I to take it that I have appointed the King of England, the Kaiser of Germany, the Emperor of all the Russias and the Sultan of Turkey? And all are equally entitled, under divine sanction, to the obedience of their subjects? Which means that I have raised several armies of obedient citizens, all of whom are bound to obey, just to run a war for My amusement? Did I appoint Hitler? Mussolini? Idi Amin? Ronald Reagan?

Well, no—not Ronald Reagan!

You see what a ridiculous notion this is, that civil authorities derive their right to be obeyed from Me?

Which laws have I ordained that you will obey? The laws of apartheid? Laws that discriminate against women or anyone else for that matter? Laws that command you to go to war to kill people you have never met, against whom you hold no grudge?

You humans are totally inconsistent on this matter

---

[18] Romans 13:1

of obedience to the civil authorities. You make all sorts of fine pronouncements about how it is no excuse for atrocious behaviour to say that you were 'only obeying orders'—but on the other hand you maintain that the loyal citizen has no option when it comes to obeying orders, because ultimately they come from Me. Is this not ridiculous?

That's all very well, but if we let people pick and choose which laws they will obey and which they will ignore we will have anarchy.

Nonsense. Most people will obey the good laws because they are self-evidently in the interests of a harmonious, peaceful community. People will even tolerate the marginal rules—the ones that are obviously the work of meddling kings and politicians, like wearing bicycle helmets, because it is not worth playing the martyr by flouting them. But ultimately, you, as an individual, must accept responsibility for your actions and the Nuremberg principle is a good one. It is no excuse to say that you were only obeying orders.

So I come back to My original point. Most of the nine million casualties in the First World War ultimately have themselves to blame. They should have refused to go— it's as simple as that.

Simple? Let me tell You it would take courage to resist the herd instinct once the bugles start to play . . .

More courage than it takes to get out of a trench and run towards machine-guns?

Well, yes—now You come to mention it. I suppose, for some peculiar reason it would take more courage.

You mean it takes *less* courage to go to certain death than it does to risk the scorn of your neighbours? You humans really are a very peculiar species. It's probably just as well that there is no one else quite like you anywhere in the universe. You are like an entire species of infants!

You said something a moment ago about not objecting to being held responsible for the writings of Shaw. As a matter of interest, do You actually 'inspire' authors or composers or painters?

Of course not. Shaw's idea of holding the pen for the Life Force is a charming one, but what he wrote came from his own experience and imagination. Personally, I would have given *Pygmalion* a much happier ending. Higgins should have come down off his high horse and married Eliza and gone into parliament as a socialist reformer. Alfie Doolittle could have been his electorate secretary and organiser and Colonel Pickering could have become a pacifist and campaigned against the iniquitous impositions of the Versaille treaty. How am I doing?

Well, to tell the truth—and since You are God you probably already know what I am thinking—I don't think that Your additions would improve the original much, do You?

Oh?

Look, I hope that I haven't hurt Your feelings.

Don't be ridiculous! Anyway, what you really want to know is if all or any of the Bible is the 'inspired Word of God'. Now, let me ask you something. If you sat down to write a book and when you had finished you took it to the publisher and said: 'Right! Here it is. The inspired word of God!' What sort of reaction would you expect?

Well . . .

Exactly! And have you ever read the 'inspired word of God'? Take a look at the books of Joshua and Judges. Sit down and read them right through without stopping and tell me what you think. These two books are simply catalogues of the most appalling atrocities committed by the invading Israelites—whole towns and

areas laid waste and every living thing, animals as well
as humans, slaughtered. And I am supposed to be responsible for this! Not only responsible, but highly
delighted!

Can we backtrack a little and pick up the question
again of why it is that Christianity is such a bloodthirsty
religion?

Yes, of course . . .

There is a fatal flaw which runs right through Judaism
and Christianity, and Islam too, for that matter—it is
the delusion of 'chosen-ness'. You see, once you delude
yourselves that I have 'chosen' you for some reason or
other, then you immediately designate the rest of humanity as un-chosen or rejected—literally, godforsaken.
Therefore, all those who are outside the chosen people
are less than human and fair game, as it were.

The shocking atrocities which are reported with pride
in the Old Testament are justified on the grounds that
I have already rejected the victims, so it is no loss to
anyone if they are murdered. Indeed, it will make the
world a place more congenial to Me.

The New Testament refines this concept of chosen-
ness from a primitive hereditary delusion to a more
subtle and voluntary one. Jesus is supposed to have
said this:

> When the Son of man comes in all his glory, and all the
> angels with him, then he will sit on his glorious throne.
> Before him will be gathered all the nations and he will
> separate them one from another as a shepherd separates
> the sheep from the goats, and he will place the sheep at
> his right hand, but the goats at the left. Then the king
> will say to those at his right hand: 'Come, O blessed of
> my Father, inherit the kingdom prepared for you from the
> foundation of the world . . .' Then he will say to those at
> his left hand: 'Depart from me, you cursed, into the eternal
> fire prepared for the devil and his angels . . .' And they

will go away into eternal punishment, but the righteous into eternal life.[19]

Now it goes without saying that if you think of human beings as belonging to two categories, like sheep and goats, with one lot marked out for eternal pleasure and the others for eternal torment then you have clearly got My permission to do whatever you like to the goats, haven't you? All through the New Testament you will find this division of people into the twin categories of the 'righteous' and the 'cursed'; the orthodox and the heretics; the believers and the infidels; Catholics and Protestants; us and them. John's gospel is entirely to do with 'the Jews' against everyone and everything that is good and decent and godly. This dividing of the world into the good and the bad; the blessed and the cursed; the godly and the infidel; the believer and the pagan; the saved and the damned is, and always has been, the fatal flaw at the heart of Christianity. It is the arrogant assumption that there is only one way to Me and that your little subsect knows what it is that has lead to wars, witch-hunts, pogroms, inquisitions and *autos de fé*. Do you know what an *auto de fé* is?

Well, sort of . . .

An *auto de fé*, literally, means 'act of faith'. In fact, what it was was the burning of heretics at the stake. It usually happened on a Sunday. The heretics were paraded through the town in funny smocks (called *sanbenitos*) and hats and had to endure interminable sermons about orthodoxy while tied to the stake waiting for the faggots to be lit. If one of them had a sudden change of heart and repented his wicked ways he was granted a boon. He was strangled before the fire was lit. Those who were obdurate in their heresy, even after torture to near death,

---

[19] Matthew 25:31

were slowly burned. It was looked upon as a rehearsal for judgment day.

There was always the possibility that some poor sod would confess to anything under torture. So even the Inquisitor acknowledged that the occasional innocent and totally orthodox believer would find herself being roasted alive. Never mind, they said. 'What a glorious death! To die for the Faith and in the Faith. They would go straight to paradise. Of what had they to complain?'[20]

Incidentally, the Inquisition was a nice little earner for the monarchy in Spain. The property of *suspected* heretics was confiscated by the crown before the trial had even started. Not surprisingly, rich people were more at risk from the Inquisition than the poor. I suppose that that is something to be said in its favour.

The apologist for the Inquisition, Ludovico à Paramo, blamed Me for all this. He said that I set the prototype for the Inquisition when I banished Adam and Eve from the Garden of Eden and thus I confiscated their worldly goods. What's more, I made them wear fig leaves and animal skins as a sign of their sin, and this was the prototype for the *sanbenito*, the horrible smock worn by the condemned heretics on their way to the *auto de fé*.[21] You've got to give him full marks for ingenuity.

You're no doubt wondering how all this could be done in the name of the person who is supposed to have said: 'Love one another as I have loved you.'[22] Well, unhappily, that is not the last word on human/divine relations in the Bible.

There is a vision in Revelation in which a plague of locusts descends on the earth with instructions from Me 'not to harm the grass of the earth or any green growth or any tree, but only those of mankind who have

---

[20] Jean Plaidy, *The Rise of the Spanish Inquisition*, Robert Hale, London, 1977, p 154

[21] *ibid*, p 158

[22] John 13:34

not the seal of God upon their foreheads; they were allowed to torture them for five months but not to kill them, and their torture was like the torture of a scorpion when it stings a man. And in those days men will seek death and will not find it; they will long to die, and death flies from them.'[23]

This, apparently, is where Pope Innocent IV got the idea that heretics should be tortured, which he authorised in his papal bull *Ad Extirpanda* in 1252. But in fact it was as early as 380 when the Church had only recently been unbanned by the emperor, that this decree was promulgated:

> We order those who follow this law to assume the name of 'Catholic Christians'. The rest, on the other hand, whom we declare to be mad and insane, have to bear the shame of being called heretics . . . They must first be struck by the vengeance of God and then also by the punishment of our anger, for which we derive our power from the heavenly judgement.[24]

Christians have been some of the most dangerous people to be around for the past 2000 years. In fact, any unprejudiced reading of Church history would have to make a chap an atheist, there's no two ways about it. But fortunately, I am here today to put the record straight—I had nothing to do with it! Don't blame Me!

You keep saying that, but I'm not sure that it's fair. After all—You are God . . .

---

[23] Revelation 9:4
[24] Kahl, p 63

· 5 ·

Good & Evil

O*ne of the oldest theological conundrums goes something like this: If God is omnipotent and created everything then God must have created the Devil. In other words, You are responsible for evil as well as for good. May we talk about this puzzle for a while?*

Certainly. But I cannot see that there is anything puzzling about it. You talk about *evil* as though it were a palpable substance that floats around—or perhaps like a virus which infects people without their having any control over it, just like you might catch a cold.

Here we have a sort of *mass* of evil and from time to time bits break loose and mischief is done.

Now, that is superstition and you should know it.

Is there a Devil?

With or without a tail and red longjohns? Don't be ridiculous!

The theology of evil is very interesting for a detached observer like Myself—except that, of course, there is no one quite like Myself. What makes it interesting are the contradictions built into the notion of evil as an entity which is separate from the imaginations of humans.

You see, on the one hand you have the notion of individual responsibility, but over against that you propose a dark and malign power which is so effective that it can make people do things that they know are bad and which they would rather not do. So here we have people who believe that Satan or Beelzebub or Old Nick have tempted them to do something rotten, yet they still accept that they ought to have known better and, at least those who worry about these things, do not try to excuse themselves on the grounds that they were only obeying the commands of the Lord of the Flies. Except for Paul, of course. He had it all figured out.

> I can will what is right, but I cannot do it. For I do not do the good I want, but the evil I do not want is what I do. Now if I do what I do not want it is no longer I that do it, but sin which dwells within me.[1]

Do you have any idea what he was on about? Was he absolving himself from all responsibility for his actions on the grounds that there was some mysterious evil force called *sin* which had him under its control?

I'm afraid I don't know. Seeing that You are supposed

---

[1] Romans 7:18–20

to have inspired the words I assumed that You would know.

I thought that I had told you about that inspiration stuff. What Paul wrote is nothing to do with me.

This is very curious—because if the Devil is as potent as Christian mythology has it then no one would be able to resist him, and everyone would have a ready-made excuse for appalling behaviour. You would only have to say: 'The Devil made me do it' and everyone would understand and forgive. But it doesn't work like that, does it?

But, to take a clichéd example, people point to the Nazis and say: 'Look at that, you can't escape the reality of the existence of evil . . .'

What on earth does that mean? Do you want to talk about Hitler in particular?

Well, he is usually set up these days as the perfect example of evil personified.

Do you know that the truly depressing thing about Hitler was his ordinariness. His vanities were banal. Like any person who aspires to political leadership he believed that he had some unique formula which would make Germany rich and powerful and the envy of the world. He was a very ordinary racist who believed that, on the whole, an homogeneous society is preferable to a cosmopolitan one. He subscribed to conspiracy theories and sought out scapegoats for punishment. I can name a bunch of other political leaders whom you would immediately identify as perfectly respectable or even great leaders whose motivations were exactly the same as Hitler's. You must understand, he was not an exceptional man.

But he lived in exceptional times when the technology at his disposal made it possible for him to live out his fantasies—and as his fantasies were shared by most of his compatriots he was not constrained by any internal resistance. And he was confident that the technological

superiority which he thought he enjoyed would overwhelm any external resistance. In other words, he was
an ordinary person who had total, 100 per cent permission to live out his delusions of grandeur.

Another thing to bear in mind is that if you persist
in treating Hitler as an exceptional example then you
will overlook the Hitlerishness of national leaders whose
crimes may not be on the same magnitude but whose
motives are not all that different. Just remember that
most misery and pain in the world has been caused by
people who were convinced that they were doing good.
Most happiness has been caused by people who mind
their own business because they are too modest to presume that they know what is best for anyone else.

An American judge had some words to say on the
threat posed by people whose intentions are good and
honourable:

> Experience should teach us to be more on our guard to
> protect liberty when the government's purposes are bene-
> ficent. The greatest dangers to liberty lurk in the insidious
> encroachments by men of zeal, well meaning but without
> understanding.[2]

For some reason people cannot see that even the worst
tyrants act under the delusion that they are doing good.
The idea that Hitler actually thought exactly the same
as Churchill—namely that he was a great humanitarian
and a noble leader—is something that few people want
to, or are able to, grasp. But consider Stalin. There you
see the contradiction more starkly. The man who murdered millions and also lead his people to a great victory
over the Nazis was presumably not aware of any dis-
continuity of motive. He was always doing good. That
was his intention.

---

[2] Justice Brandeis *Olmstead v United States* 277 US 438 (1928)

What's more, respected and influential Christians who were Hitler's contemporaries agreed with him that he was doing a power of good in the world.

In 1941 the Church presidents and Bishops of Saxony, Mecklenburg, Schleswig-Holstein, the Anhalt of Saxony, Thüringen and Lübeck published the following declaration:

> The National Socialists leaders of Germany have provided indisputable documentary evidence that the Jews are responsible for this war in its world-wide magnitude. They have therefore made the necessary decisions and taken the necessary steps, both internal and external, to ensure that the life of the German nation is protected against Judaism.
>
> As members of that same German nation, the undersigned leaders of the German Evangelical church stand in the forefront of this historical struggle to defend our country, because of which it has been necessary for the national police to issue a statement to the effect that the Jews are enemies of the German nation and of the world, just as it was also necessary for Dr Martin Luther to demand, on the basis of his own bitter experience, that the severest measures should be taken against the Jews . . .[3]

And what, exactly, did Dr Martin Luther have to say on the subject of Jews?

We Christians can hardly believe that a Jew's foul mouth is worthy to speak the name of God in our presence and

---

[3] This statement by the Church leaders is quoted in Joachim Kahl's *The Misery of Christianity*, who shows how a straight line can be drawn from John's Gospel to the Third Reich through the entire history of Christian anti-Semitism. Kahl argues that John's Gospel is the earliest anti-Semitic tract that we have, in which the villains are constantly referred to as 'the Jews', without any attempt being made to distinguish between individuals. It is John who goes to the greatest lengths to excuse Pilate for his part in the execution of Jesus. Pilate 'went out to the Jews again and said: "I find no crime in him." ' In chapters 18 and 19 of John the collective expression 'the Jews' is used twenty-one times.

if any one of us should hear a Jew speak that name, he
should at once inform the authorities or else throw pig
shit at him . . .

Julius Streicher, the editor of the Nazi paper *Der Stürmer*,
quoted Luther in his defence at Nuremberg.

Luther also coined the expression 'A woman's place
is in the home'—did you know that? And he wasn't at
all fussed if a woman had so many children that she
eventually died from sheer child-bearing exhaustion. 'If
they become tired or even die, it does not matter. Let
them die in childbirth—that is why they are there.'
Charming!

Dr Martin Luther is famous for saying at the Diet
of Worms: 'I cannot and I will not recant anything, for
to go against conscience is neither right nor safe. Here
I stand. I cannot do otherwise. God help me. Amen.'

It sounds wonderfully heroic, but I do wish that he had
left Me out of it. However, there is more that you ought
to know about Dr Luther. It was he who established in
the German mind that before all else they owed obedience
to the state. Those words of Paul from Romans which
you have already mentioned were taken literally by
Luther and he turned them into the first commandment.

Let every person be subject to the governing authorities.
For there is no authority except from God, and those that
exist have been instituted by God. Therefore he who resists
the authorities resists what God has appointed, and those
who resist will incur judgment.[4]

You have already pointed out that many people think
that one of life's most important rules is to always obey
the government—but one moment's reflection will tell
you that that is a ridiculous rule. Who were the heroes
in Hitler's Germany—those who obeyed the government

---

[4] Romans 13:1–2

or those who opposed it? The majority of Germans were of the opinion that you should always obey the government. Martin Luther set that up as a moral absolute when he gave permission to the secular authorities to slaughter the peasants at the end of the peasants' war. And I mean *slaughter*. These were not people killed in the heat of battle. Tens of thousands of peasants who had surrendered their arms were systematically slaughtered. Luther was shocked at the magnitude of the murder, but it was too late to be shocked. He had already given permission for it to happen when he wrote:

> If the peasant is in open rebellion, then he is outside the law of God, for rebellion is not simply murder, but it is like a great fire which attacks and lays waste the land . . . Therefore let everyone who can, smite, slay, and stab, secretly or openly, remembering that nothing can be more poisonous, hurtful or devilish than a rebel. It is just as when one must kill a mad dog; if you don't strike him, he will strike you and the whole land with you.

But then when 100 000 'mad dogs' were put to the sword, Luther sent out another pamphlet in which he admitted that he had said that the peasants' ears needed to be 'unbuttoned with bullets', but he didn't mean that the victors should show no mercy to captives.[5]

Well, it was too late, wasn't it? And the earlier pamphlet was the one that left the lasting impression. In fact you could say that 400 years later the chickens well and truly came home to roost.

In fact, Luther left the Germans with a deadly combination—he sanctified obedience and taught contempt for Jews.

---

[5] You can read about Martin Luther and the peasants' revolt in Roland Bainton's *Here I Stand* (Abingdon Press, New York, 1960). Naturally, the Catholic princes held Luther responsible for the revolt. If the peasants were stirred into rebelling against the rule of the Church, they reasoned, you could hardly expect them to respect the rule of the state.

This is one of the mysteries of life for us. How could a cultured, civilised people in the middle of the twentieth century go on such an orgy of destruction and murder? It is as though all morality was suspended and everything was permitted.

Permission is the key word in understanding why people behave wickedly and apparently without remorse. Why don't you go down to the bank with a gun and steal all the money that they have on the premises?

I might get caught!

Exactly. You have not been given permission by the community in which you live to rob banks.

But let's imagine that you can go down there and rob the bank, certain that you will get away with it. I will look after you. You won't be caught, I promise. Now, off you go. What is there to stop you?

I don't know. I suppose that there is some sort of taboo on robbing banks that I can't bring myself to break.

You are up against the universal imperative. If everyone robbed banks then an important stabilising factor in society would be destroyed and your community would degenerate into a tribe of paranoid bank-robbers. In other words, the thing that stops you robbing the bank is the instinctive feeling that to do so could lead to chaos and that you yourself may be destroyed in the chaos. So, in the end you decline to do the 'wrong' thing and choose to do the 'right' thing for reasons of self-preservation.

To put it at its most basic, you will not rob the bank because your genes will not let you. It would be an act of individual and group suicide. Your genes will not give you *permission* to commit acts which endanger their survival and their chances of replication in the next generation of humans.

But it is ironic that while permission for people to rob banks is withheld, permission to commit much worse crimes is often given. So, for instance, in 1945 in England no one had permission to rob a bank, but many thousands of men were given permission to utterly destroy the city of Dresden and all the people living in it.

Now you may say, quite rightly, that this was temporary permission given in special circumstances. But it was not a once-only moral phenomenon. In the town of Amarillo in Texas nuclear warheads are made. The Roman Catholic bishop of this town has told his flock that I do *not* give permission for them to engage in this activity, any more than I give permission for the robbing of banks.

(Actually, I don't give permission for anything, as you know, but the bishop still thinks in the old-fashioned way and if I am to be held responsible for anything then I would rather be held responsible for what he says I say than for what many of his ecclesiastical colleagues have claimed to have heard from Me.)

What is interesting about this is that genetically the warmongers are right. Their genes give them the message: it is okay to kill first in order to survive. Then their priests provide a pseudo-religious vindication of their murderous deeds. It takes an act of moral originality to rise above this limited view of survival and say: 'Hold on a moment. What is at stake here is the survival of the entire genetic wealth of the planet. We are not talking gazelles and lions here, where at most one or two gene repositories are in danger. We are not even talking about a single human tribe, or even a nation. We are talking about every single gene of every kind being in danger. We will have to rethink permission and prohibition. We need new moral imperatives to suit the new technologies of death.'

So what was wrong with Hitler's genes?

Nothing. It was more that he had faulty information which the genes processed incorrectly. He fervently believed that his best genetic bet was to conquer Europe and exterminate the inferior races. Because his combination of information and genetic imperative is so at odds with yours you think that you need a devil to explain what happened. Nonsense!

And Hitler had permission, both from the people and the priests, to go on the warpath. He was unrestrained.

The thing about the Hitler phenomenon which I find hardest to understand is that the man was apparently devoid of pity. It is as though he didn't have a conscience. He must have been aware every day that his orders were bringing about the deaths of thousands—eventually accumulating to millions. Yet it doesn't seem to have disturbed him.

It happens all the time. When American presidents or British prime ministers unleash their war machines on other nations they do not lose a minute's sleep over the effect that they are having on individual human beings. There is a genetic defect in those who aspire to lead nations. The pity gene is missing. Or perhaps it has been replaced by a double quota of vanity genes. Look around at your national leaders. Can you name a compassionate one? Indeed, can you name one who is not ruthless?

Human societies, until very recently, were ruled over by the man (almost always the man) who won control in the never-ending process of intrigue, war and assassination. This is still a method of selecting the king in many places, but in those tribes which have aspired to *civilisation* other processes, usually called democracy, have been invented for the selection of kings. But to succeed in democracy you must be no less ruthless than was necessary when the king was the man who triumphed in combat. The only real difference is that in a contest where wit is more important than brute force it is possible for a physically weak man or a woman to win the contest and become the monarch.

There are those who believe that if the world were governed by women it would be a kinder, softer place.

This is a vain hope. Not because women may not be, on the whole, softer and kinder creatures—it is a vain hope because the *process* of king-making will not change to accommodate the gender. The person who fights to gain control and wins will be ruthless and generally defective in the pity gene. Let's face it, some of the most ruthless and bloodthirsty rulers of your century have been women.

Kind and compassionate people rarely get to be president or prime minister. And ruthless rulers will do whatever they think they can get away with. They are the human equivalent of the successful bull seal or moose or elephant. They get the run of the harem.

The way you talk about the genetic predisposition to do good or bad things makes it sound as though humans have no choice about how they behave.

You certainly have fewer choices than you think you do. The only safe approach to morality seems to be a very stern attitude to your own responsibilities and a very forgiving attitude to others.

We should forgive Hitler?

Well, perhaps not forgiving—how about understanding. After all, Hitler didn't get up every morning and say to himself: 'Let's see. What wickedness can I commit today? How about invading Poland? That's really terrifically evil and will give me tremendous pleasure.'

In fact, he got up every morning and said: 'What glorious deed can I do today for my tribe? I know—I will order the invasion of Poland. This will do wonders for national self-esteem. It will also right old wrongs and in the process will open up living room for our overcrowded nation. Today I will do an immense amount of good. People will thank me for a thousand years to come.'

Most of the monumental evil in the world is done by men labouring under the delusion that they were striving for the common good. Indeed, just as a principle to live by, you might bear this in mind. Any politician who tells you that he is doing something for the good of the nation is almost certain to be lying—but that doesn't mean that he doesn't believe what he's saying. He does! And that's what makes him dangerous.

You make it sound as if all our national leaders are mad . . .

There is some truth in that.

Most of us—like about 99.99 per cent of us—will never become kings or queens. So what do the concepts of good and evil mean for ordinary people? Is it all in the genes?

Mostly, yes. Most human behaviour is judged to be good or evil because of the effect that it has on the prospect for genetic survival. Let Me give you an example, first from the animals. Consider the case of Thomson's gazelle.

When a lion comes near a herd of Thomson's gazelles, the animals that sense the predator's proximity start to bounce up and down on the spot. It's called 'stotting' and you humans have tended to interpret this behaviour as a self-sacrificing act of altruistic goodness. But consider this. What is really happening is that the stotting gazelles are saying to the lion: Look at me! Look how high I can jump! And I can run like the wind—so there's no point wasting your energies trying to catch me. Go for one of those others with their heads down munching the grass. They're easy catches.[6]

The point of this story is that it really makes no sense

[6] Richard Dawkins in his book *The Selfish Gene* (OUP, Oxford, 1976, p 90), writes about the theories of the Israeli biologist Zahavi, who has re-interpreted the gazelle's behaviour as selfish rather than altruistic. Dawkins talks about the gazelle behaviour in an interview in *More than Meets the Ear*, by Terry Lane (ABC Books (revised edition), 1991, pp 238ff).

to ascribe moral values to the gazelle's behaviour. Whether it is acting altruistically or selfishly is not important, except for the light that it throws on human behaviour. If the gazelle is acting selfishly then that is all right, because it is preserving its own genes. If it is acting altruistically then that is also all right, because it is obeying some imperative to preserve the larger gene pool represented by the herd.

Now, in human beings the instinctual responses are much the same. The most powerful instinct is the urge to survive. But sometimes that comes into conflict with other genetic imperatives. For instance, your house may be on fire and inside is your infant child. Self-preservation says: Don't go into that inferno. But the powerful urge to preserve the genetic inheritance in your child (you call it 'love') forces you to override the imperative to self-preservation. If the altruistic instinct does not overwhelm the selfish instinct then you may be the subject of moral opprobrium. You will be called a coward—which is a moral judgment. If you rush into the house and are burned to a crisp then you will be a hero—another moral judgment. And yet neither action is truly, 100 per cent voluntary. In the circumstances one genetic imperative or the other will triumph and judgment will be passed on your action as though you were a free moral agent.

In the case of the gazelle, if it is true that stotting is an entirely selfish act, we don't pass moral judgment on the animal. And if it is an altruistic act—if we can use that word—we don't assume that the gazelle is brave. We assume that it is acting instinctively. Well, much human behaviour comes into the same category.

But that makes it sound as though we are entirely predestined—that we have no control over our actions.

As I said before, you must act as though *you* are entirely responsible for everything you do, but you must regard other humans as being nearly as limited in their choices

as gazelles are. However, having said all that I want
to get back to the notions of permission and pity.

We have already talked about how religion gives permission for acts of savagery which would never pass
normal moral scrutiny. Let's consider the contradictions
in the Old Testament. On the one hand there is the
set of ten rules that Moses claimed to get from Me. Can
you imagine Me being so insecure that I need to write
a rule reminding everyone that I am the only God and
that you'd better not go worshipping anyone else? That
is the sort of rule a politician would write, not a God.

However, that is a trivial rule. The most important
of the ten is the one that says: You shall not kill. This
is a good rule—as are the rules about not stealing, lying
or committing adultery. They are all good rules to have
in a community because if killing, lying or adultery were
not taboo then the trust essential for the continuance
of the community would be non-existent and the community would eventually perish. This would be devas-
tating for the genes, which would lose opportunities for
self-replication and immortality.

However, it will not have escaped your notice, and
I have already mentioned it in passing, that the followers
of Moses were killers on a grand scale. When they arrived
in the land of Canaan there were already tribes in resi-
dence. I am supposed to have told Saul: 'Now go and
smite Amalek, and utterly destroy all that they have; do
not spare them, but kill both man and woman, infant
and suckling, ox and sheep, camel and ass.'[7] So what
Moses really meant in his ten rules was this: there will
be no killing until I give permission—and then you will
do it with enthusiasm. And all societies proceed in this
way. They have a general taboo against random killing
which is overridden by the right of the priestly class

---

[7] This story is in 1 Samuel 15:3. There are many more like it in the Old
Testament.

to give permission to kill. Then the citizen has not only the right but also the duty to kill and to do it with enthusiasm.

Are there any absolute moral rules? After all, if the rule against murder is conditional and circumstantial, what about the others?

There are no moral absolutes—or at least if you want to have some then that's all right, but don't hold Me responsible for them. Even the prohibition on murder may be overridden in some circumstances, but you cannot possibly say in advance what they might be.

Here is an historical case for you to consider. During your Second World War the resistance fighters in France who called themselves *Maquis* lived every day by telling lies, stealing and killing. They survived on false passports, false identification papers and ration cards. They stole food and supplies. They killed Germans, collaborators and even, on occasion, members of their own band who might have been captured, tortured and forced to expose the resistance movement. A group of *Maquis* were asked if this meant that everything is permitted. 'Yes, everything is permitted—and everything is forbidden.'[8]

You make it sound as though the end justifies the means . . .

Well, what else can? Lenin's reply to those who argued that the end should not justify the means was: 'If the end does not justify the means, then in the name of sanity and justice, *what does?*'

That's all very well, but how do we then judge what ends justify what means?

What you are asking for is a catalogue of ends, divided

---

[8] Joseph Fletcher tells this story in *Situation Ethics* (SCM Press, London, 1966, p 124).

into good and bad ends. Then you can look up the end in question and if it's a good one you can murder someone to achieve it. On the other hand, if the end is a bad one then you wouldn't even tell a little fib to achieve it. That's ridiculous because it is never so clear cut.

Well, it would help if we had a few straightforward rules to be going on with. That's why the Ten Commandments have had such a central position in Judaism and Christianity.

What? Even though you pick and choose when the commandment against killing will apply?

Why do you humans try so hard to avoid responsibility? Why do you hanker for iron-clad rules and iron-fisted rulers? You must know, as a matter of commonsense, that there are no rules that you can apply in all places, at all times and in all circumstances. If the meaning of life is Life, then you must be obliged to act in ways that will give Life its best chance of continuing. And who knows what that might imply in some situations. Generally speaking, it is no doubt true that life will get on best where people don't lie, steal, cheat or kill. And as a general rule it is advisable to obey the laws of the community just for the sake of tranquillity and harmony. Indeed, these general principles are so obvious that you need really convincing reasons and arguments to go against them or to ride roughshod over them. But you can't seriously defend the principle that unjust laws should be obeyed; or that allegiance should be pledged to tyrants; or that you should obey the orders of presidents or prime ministers just because they happen to occupy those particular positions. Even where the governors govern by the consent of the governed, individual responsibility is not put into suspension until the next election.

That's all very well, but if morality is dependent on circumstances how can we tell the difference between right and wrong?

Ultimately, in the most difficult situations, you will never know. You can't blame Me. You can't say: God told me to do it! And you can't refer to precedent, because you will find that either there isn't one or your claim to be acting according to precedent will sound insufferably arrogant. I mean, if you say, well, I'm going to defy the government on this issue because Jesus defied the authorities of his time, then you are making an outrageous bid for vindication of your actions.

There is a church song that goes:

Once to every man and nation
Comes the moment to decide
In the strife of truth with falsehood
For the good or evil side . . .

It is usually sung to the same tune as *Deutschland über alles*—is this intentional?

I don't know—but look, I would like to go back to where we were talking about the crimes that have been committed by true believers in Your name. And You say we can't defend them on the grounds that no one knew any better?

That's right.

Well, it could also be argued that these misguided people were not real Christians.

Good grief, that's even more ridiculous than saying that they were children of their times. Who is going to seriously argue that Martin Luther wasn't a *real* Christian? He even has a whole sect named after him. Or that the popes who revelled in the Inquisition weren't 'real Christians'. Or that the Grand Inquisitor of Spain, Tomas de Torquemada, was not a real Christian. He was such a real Christian that he sent 10 220 people to the stake and 97 371 to the galleys for various

forms of heresy. You can't get any more real than
that.[9]

In the thirteenth century Pope Innocent III—a real
Christian, if ever there was one—proclaimed a crusade
against fellow Christians, the Cathars of southern France.
The wars against the Cathari heretics between 1208
and 1244 are known as the Albigensian wars, and I
mention them because I got involved in a very interesting
way.

Orders were given that when a town was attacked every
man, woman and child was to be killed. When someone
objected that even amongst heretics you might find a
true-believer or two, the answer was given: 'Kill them
all, God will know His own.'

No prisoners were taken. Anyone captured was killed
at once. The Pope's crusaders were promised they could
have as much booty as they could carry. The cities of
southern France were pillaged and a mild, liberal
civilisation was wiped out in a terrible bloodbath. The
Papal legate on the spot to keep an ecclesiastical eye
on proceedings reported his satisfaction to Rome: 'God's
wrath (Me again!) has raged in wondrous wise against
the city of Béziers.' Hundreds of thousands of people
perished, including the musicians, the troubadours, who
were the glory of the Cathari civilisation.[10]

It was another pope, Innocent IV—another true Christian—who laid down the rules for torture of heretics.
For instance, no one could be tortured more than once,
but the followers of the good Saint Dominic—another
genuine Christian, you must admit—got around that.
They never tortured a heretic more than once—they
merely *suspended* the process for a few hours and then
continued the same torture. But don't think for a moment that they were motivated by anything other than

[9] Kahl, p 68
[10] Walter Nigg, *The Heretics*, Dorset, London, 1949, pp 190–1

Christian love. The torture instruments were regularly sprinkled with holy water.

What did the Cathars believe? It must have been something really offensive, surely, for the Pope to wage such a savage war against them.

The Cathars were dualists. They believed that I had two sons—one good, Christ, and one bad, Satan. In fact, they believed that two powers, one good and one satanic, were both eternal and your world was made by the bad one. They reckoned that the greatest sin in this worst of all possible worlds was reproduction and the only way to get in My good books was by repentance, asceticism and 'consolation', which was a ritual a bit like baptism. After consolation a person was perfect, as long as she didn't eat milk, meat or eggs and abstained from sex.

Hardly sounds a good reason to kill hundreds of thousands of them.

Ah—but you see what they were being killed for was not essentially to do with what they believed.

The heretics were killed because they dared to think differently and to entertain improper opinions. And by all accounts they were prosperous, peaceful, sophisticated and contented. Jealousy played no small part in their downfall.

The struggle for the right to march to a different drummer has gone on as long as humans have thought for themselves. But it is ironic, is it not, that it is the three monotheistic religions that claim to have personal contact with Me which are most intolerant of dissent or deviance?

Even when the 'heresy' is held in utter ignorance by pagans who have never even heard of Jesus, let alone *homo-ousion*, the fury of the Church can be uncontained. When the conquistadors were overrunning the new world and introducing the 'Indians' to the benefits of Christianity, they carried with them this proclamation:

God the Lord has delegated to Peter and his successors all power over all people of the earth, so that all people must obey the successors of Peter. Now one of these popes has made a gift of the newly discovered islands and countries [in America] and everything that they contain to the kings of Spain, so that, by virtue of this gift, their majesties are now kings and lords of all these islands and of the continent. You are therefore required to recognise Holy church as mistress and ruler of the whole world and to pay homage to the Spanish king as your new lord. Otherwise, we shall, with God's help, proceed against you with violence and force you under the yoke of the Church and the king, treating you as rebellious vassals deserve to be treated. We shall take your property away from you and make your women and children slaves. At the same time, we solemnly declare that only you will be to blame for the bloodshed and the disaster that will overtake you.[11]

I suppose that you could say that they had been warned. Although whether or not they understood the language in which the warning was written is doubtful.

The ferocity of the affronted Church was even greater when it was turned against other Christians. In the sixteenth century Philip II of Spain sent his trusted general, the Duke of Alva, to the Netherlands to stamp out the Protestant heresy there. Alva convened the infamous 'Council of Blood' to track down and exterminate the apostates. He went about his work with a will. Philip helped by pronouncing the death sentence on the entire population of Holland! This was a touch extravagant, even by the standards of the day, but Alva boasted himself that he was responsible for the executions of 18 600 people, which is not a bad score.[12]

In the case of Torquemada we know how many people

---

[11] Kahl, pp 48–9
[12] Jean Plaidy, *The Rise of the Spanish Inquisition*, Robert Hale, London, 1977, p 373

he was responsible for killing—and we also know the torture methods used to extract confessions of heresy and the naming of associates—because the Inquisition kept such meticulous records.

In the nineteenth century the priest Juan Antonio Llorente was such a respected man in civil and religious circles that he was given a seat on the Supreme Council of Seville. He then became the Commissary of the Holy Office and was required to provide proof that he had no Jewish or Moorish blood in his veins. This made him suspicious about what was going on in the Church. His superiors sent him off to a monastery to do penance for his curiosity. But by this time he had had the chance to go through the archives of the Inquisition. He blew the whistle!

Needless to say, Llorente didn't do any better than other whistle-blowers, but he was lucky that he didn't try it a couple of hundred years earlier. As it was, he was unfrocked and forced to flee from Spain and he settled in France where he proceeded to tell the world what the Inquisition had been doing for the past 500 years.[13]

So you see it was when the Christian church held undisputed, totalitarian sway over all of Europe that it was most dangerous to be a woman, a Jew, a dissenter or an Arab. Don't you think that you should consider, as I have suggested, that Christianity itself is a seriously flawed religion?

---

[13] *ibid*, pp 121–2

· 6 ·

Is There Life after Death?

*I*s there life after death?

I can answer that quite categorically. Yes and no!

Yes and no?

That's right. Yes, there is and no, there isn't. If you mean does your little ego take flight from the dying body and go off to some other part of the universe where it can have a good time (or suffer terribly, depending on how you have behaved on earth) then the answer is no.

You get one go at life and that's it. No reincarnation. No Heaven. No Hell. When it's over it's over. And, as one of your countrymen has said on many occasions, when you come to terms with that fact of death you will find it a great aphrodisiac for life.[1]

But many people have reported having strange near-death experiences which have convinced them that they were setting out on some glorious journey to another place as they were dying.

Well, they would, wouldn't they? Imagine what must be going on in a brain as it closes down? There must be all sorts of dream-like visions created in the critical moment of death. You will have noticed that all these visions are very terrestrial. There are always bright lights and leafy glades and lots of other people dressed in white—all the conventional anthropomorphic pictures of the afterlife that you could expect to come floating up from the subconscious at this critical cerebral moment.

Let's assume that your ego did persist after death, do you really expect it to be dressed in white and spend eternity lying around in a leafy glade on a glorious spring afternoon with bright lights shining and heavenly music playing? Does this not strike you as childish?

A friend of mine once told me of his near-death experience. He had had a heart attack and just as the ambulance men arrived he started to leave his body. He felt himself rising to the ceiling, looking down in a detached way at what was happening in the room as the men tried to restart his heart with the electric heart-starter. And he heard voices, too.

What did they say?

Well, I'm a bit embarrassed to tell You this . . .

---

[1] *This is one of Phillip Adams' oft-quoted aphorisms.*

Come on—I think I can take it.

They said: 'Oh shit! The fucking battery's flat.'[2]

This is not a very encouraging near-death experience—but it has the ring of authenticity about it.

A lot of religion is the result of cowardice. Humans cannot accept the fact that one day they will die and, for most of you, it will be as though you have never existed. Except for one thing.

You do achieve a sort of immortality through the persistence of your genes. If you have offspring then some part of you will go on. But even that is not a great consolation because every generation of your descendants will carry only a diluted version of your genes.

Why did You make us so that we had to die? According to the Bible we only have to die because Eve went and picked the forbidden fruit. If it hadn't been for her we would live forever.

I think that I can take it for granted that you don't really believe that. The birth, decay and death of organisms is built into the system of the universe. There's no point in whingeing about it or hoping that it won't be true for you. It is true for every living creature. I know that some humans feel that it is not fair that turtles and trees live for hundreds of years, but that's just the way it is.

Let me ask you something—do you think that chimpanzees go on living after they die?

I don't suppose they do. If they did then we would have to imagine that all creatures go on living after they die—and for spiders that's a bit hard to swallow.

I have heard it said that humans and chimpanzees share the same genes, except for a mere 2 per cent. So if humans

---

[2] This story was told to me by the late Peter Evans, much-loved presenter of the 3LO breakfast program.

are to go on living after death when you don't expect chimpanzees to do the same it must mean that in the 2 per cent of genes that you don't share with chimps is the gene for immortality. Does that sound very likely?

I suppose not.

If I were in your shoes I would be telling your children, as soon as they are old enough to understand, that they haven't got all that long to live and that therefore they should be planning to use the time available for the best possible results. It amazes me that humans always live as though they were going to live forever. Then someone says: What would you do if you knew you were going to die next Thursday? And suddenly people seem to have a list of things that they have been putting off that they would get stuck into in the seven days remaining. But why wait until the dreaded prognosis?

I suppose because most of us are taught from an early age not to indulge ourselves like that. We are told that we should save for a rainy day and generally put off having a good time until some unspecified time in the future.

Ah yes. Well that's a peculiarly human problem, isn't it? You can imagine a future, which other animals can't, and so you put a lot of energy into planning and generally putting things off instead of living for the day. Remember Jesus said that you shouldn't fret about tomorrow, today is enough to be getting on with.

Excuse me, You've . . .

I know, I've ended a sentence with prepositions again. Who cares? I'm only God, you know—I'm not a pedant.

Humans seem to spend more time thinking about what they are going to do and what the consequences might be and whether they ought to do this or something else and in the end they do nothing and then they die complaining that they haven't done this, that or the other.

There is probably a sociobiological explanation for this perverse behaviour. The whole 'tribe' will, in a sense, go on living forever. And it is in the interests of tribal survival that individuals postpone their own gratifications until it is too late for anything but regrets. That is the origin of the taboo on the 'if it feels good, do it' rule. We characterise certain types of behaviour as 'selfish' or 'greedy', thereby passing moral judgment on them. But looked at objectively you would have to say that the only sensible way to live, from a personal point of view, is selfishly. You only get one life—so the sensible thing to do is to cram as much pleasure into it as possible.

However, we know that if selfishness were to be designated a virtue it would have a disastrous effect on the tribe as a whole. There would certainly be no more agreement about 'women and children first'. Rather the most virtuous aphorism would be, 'Every man for himself and the devil take the hindmost.' You can see how destructive this would be and how it would threaten the immortality of the genes.

So there is this everlasting tension inside you. One batch of genes is saying 'Come on. Let 'er rip. You've only got one life to live, so go for it. If it feels good, do it. You soon won't be able to.' On the other hand, there are the genetic messages implanted in you that make you put the welfare of the tribe before your personal pleasure. These little naggers say miserable things like 'Hang on! What if everyone acted the way you are planning to act? Where would we be then?'

In fact, most people would find it hard to empathise with Paul, tormented by wanting to do the right thing but always, against his will, doing the bad thing. For most humans it is probably the other way around— wanting to do the naughty thing, but restrained by the genetic imperative that we give names like 'conscience', 'duty' or 'responsibility'.

The Church has always been hostile to the 'if it feels

good, do it' philosophy. The Christian view of life seems to be that if it feels good it is almost certainly wicked. In fact given the Church's attitude to sex it's amazing that the human race has survived at all. I thought that You are a puritan?

Whatever gave you that idea?

Well, there is the story about the garden of Eden and the tree with the fruit of knowledge, which I presume means knowing all about sex—and Adam and Eve were forbidden to eat it. Then they did and they realised that they were naked and sex was invented.

You know as well as I do that that is nonsense.

Just to set the record straight, I have no opinions at all about sexual reproduction. It just happened in the course of evolutionary events. Only humans seem to find it a problem—all other species just take it for granted and get on with it. I am reliably informed that even the birds and the bees do it! Why is sexual reproduction such a source of misery for humans?

Because we are told from a very early age that it is wicked. Indeed, we get the impression that it is absolutely the naughtiest thing that a person can do and therefore has to be strictly controlled with rules about when and with whom it is okay to do it. And Saint Paul was quite clear about it, that the very topnotch Christians don't do it at all—and that You invented marriage for the weak ones who can't control themselves.

Why am I constantly being blamed for things in which I do not have the slightest interest? Do you think that I care which blue-footed frog is coupling with which blue-footed frog? So why should I be fussed about which human is having a good time with which other human?

I suppose that we like to think that we're more interesting to You than frogs.

Ah—that is the ultimate conceit. Not only do I not have any chosen people, I don't even have a chosen species. There is no reason why I should prefer your species to any other, is there?

There is a belief held by some people that we are sort of the pinnacle of creation—that evolution all leads up to us in some way, because we are the self-conscious, intelligent creatures who are capable of actually having these sorts of conversations. Doesn't that count for anything?

Well, shiver Me timbers and stab Me vitals—what a very peculiar idea. Have you ever actually observed what four billion years of evolution has produced? Rock 'n' roll! Computer games! Smart bombs! Wood chipping! *Sale of the Century*! TV commercials! The necktie! Need I go on? Can you make out any case for Me to take a special interest in the creature that produces this nonsense?

The best that we can hope for is that this is just a phase you humans are going through and that eventually you will grow out of it.

Humans are no different in essence from other creatures. You are all the creation of your genes which, as long as you have children, are the true immortals. Different genes make different robots to carry them around and to transmit them to future generations. But as for the ego or personality persisting in some other sphere of being, I'm sorry. It doesn't happen.

But we are supposed to have souls, which make us different from the other animals. And it is these souls which are supposed to leave the body at death and go and find somewhere else to live.

Really. Has anyone seen one of these souls?

No, of course not.

So what makes you think that there is such a thing as

a soul? Has anyone detected the soul with any sort of scientific implement?

No . . .

Do cows and whales have souls?

I don't suppose so. I have never heard anyone suggest that they do.

And chimpanzees . . .?

No, not as far as I know.

So at what point in the evolutionary process did *Homo sapiens* acquire a soul? At the transition point from Neanderthal man to Cro-Magnon perhaps? Somewhere in the evolutionary process humans must have acquired this peculiar characteristic which you apparently do not share with any other creatures. Did Cro-Magnon man have a soul?

Well, I don't know . . .

Or Neanderthal man? Do you think that I've got a bunch of Neanderthals up here somewhere enjoying eternal bliss—a bunch of hairy angels with beetling brows whose knuckles drag on the clouds? Do you see what you are proposing?

You know that every living creature on the earth has come about by a process which began in the Big Bang. Out of all that stardust that was flung around at the time life has emerged and organised itself into forms of ever greater complexity. And in the process one lot of genes have got themselves set up in a body with an outsize brain, rather than one with a fancy tail or great muscles for hopping.

And you are proposing that at some point in this process—fairly recently, apparently—the *Homo sapiens* branch of the evolutionary tree took a unique turning and somehow acquired a characteristic which it alone enjoys, called a soul.

But you can't tell me exactly when this is supposed to have happened and what the difference was in the creature before and after this curious development, except that presumably before it didn't have the capacity for immortality and afterwards it did.

Does that sound very probable to you?

Not when You put it that way, no. But it just doesn't seem right. Look at us. We seem too complex and extraordinary to come into being from nothing only to dissolve back into nothing in a few years. It's not enough! We want more than that.

Well, I'm afraid that there isn't any more to be had. This is the penalty you must bear for knowing more than any other creature. You know enough to be able to talk, to create literature and music and even to invent religions. You know enough to start asking the questions to which there are no answers. It's a sort of trade-off. You get the pleasures of imagination and creativity and the price you have to pay for it is existential torment.

I'll make you an offer. I'll take away the torment, but at the same time I am afraid that I have to take away Mozart. You can't have one without the other, you see. In order to know enough to be able to write, perform and appreciate great music you have to pay the price of knowing too much for your own peace of mind.

In other words, I'll make you a monkey! After all, what is a monkey but man without Mozart? Mozart comes into that 2 per cent difference in the genes. And so does existential torment. Those 2 per cent different genes are at one and the same time the glory and the misery of *Homo sapiens*. In the 2 per cent you will find music, literature, art—and unhappily religion, war and the uniquely human predisposition to murder and suicide.

Just think for a moment about life at its most basic. Consider the lilies of the field again for a moment. They toil not, neither do they spin and nor do they feel pain or have imaginations. Yet they indubitably *live*. We must presume that they are reasonably content because they don't know enough to be discontented.

Nevertheless, they are alive. There is no doubt about that. They have that vitality which makes them a little different from the earth in which they grow. Would you rather be a lily? They don't worry a lot about what is going to happen to them after they die.

No, I suppose that I wouldn't swap being a human for being a lily.

All right. Now what about a starfish? The starfish beats the lily by a small margin. It can detach itself from the ground and move around a bit. It doesn't enjoy music or art, but it has a life of sorts and is presumably contented with that life as long as there is enough around of whatever it is that starfish eat. But you don't want to be a starfish, do you?

No, I don't think so.

The starfish, at least instinctively, knows that it *can* die. I imagine that starfish instinctively recoil from anything that threatens them. This self-defence mechanism has been developed by the process of selection. The ones that jump when touched (or whatever they do) did better in the breeding and survival stakes.

Now consider the dolphin. These animals protect themselves in more elaborate ways, but presumably they cannot recognise or imagine death. They just get out of the way of danger.

Next up the ladder come humans. You can remember the deaths of others. You can imagine and anticipate your own. Like any creature with an instinct for self-preservation you will go to some lengths to avoid being killed. But you alone of all the creatures understands that no matter what you do to protect yourself, eventually and inevitably you must die. And that knowledge is a great burden on you. You desperately want it not to be true. You go to the lengths of inventing myths to wish it away.

But it won't go away. It is the great, sobering fact of life.

Is it true that You've 'set Your canon 'gainst self-slaughter'?

Of course not. It is a matter of total indifference to Me. But just as an observation, from one intelligent Being to another, it does seem that if you are smart enough to be able to imagine your own death and make all the little calculations involved in constructing a life that has some meaning for you, then you ought also to have the good sense to know when life has lost its meaning.

You humans are very inconsistent on this issue of suicide or euthanasia or whatever you want to call it. Sometimes you try to outlaw it and at other times you give medals for it.

If some poor soldier throws himself on a hand grenade to protect his comrades you give him a posthumous medal. Titus Oates kills himself by going out in the blizzard saying: 'I may be some little time . . .' and everyone knows what he is doing and his name is a byword for altruistic heroism.

But some person with a terminal illness or a crippling condition tries to kill himself and you interfere and say: 'He must just be depressed.'

Well, sometimes depression is an intelligent condition. Titus Oates was probably as depressed as it was possible to be. But that doesn't diminish the value of his sacrifice.

So why do you think that his self-killing was heroic and some quadriplegic on a life-support system who wants to die is being irrational because he is depressed?

Well, there is a conviction held by some that it's only for You to decide when a person should die.

You must be jesting. Who believes that?

The Pope, I think. Certainly his loyal followers say that is what he thinks. And he is supposed to be Your spokesman hereabouts.

That's news to Me. But suppose for a moment that he seriously holds to the view that life is entitled to run its course and that it shall not be terminated by human action—then he would have to be a pacifist and opposed to capital punishment as well as to suicide and euthanasia. Does he hold these consistent opinions?

I don't know. I assumed that it was the sort of thing that You would know. I do know that he is opposed to abortion—which raises a question about the beginning of life, rather than its end. When does life begin?

Life doesn't have a beginning. Every female born is born with a lifetime's supply of eggs already in place. Every male is born with the capacity to produce sperm. In the eggs and the sperm are the genes just waiting to move on to a new robot. Life is one continuous, unbroken thread which has no individual beginning or end.

I suppose that technically you could say that life had a beginning when the first self-replicating molecule got going in the primeval mud, but that doesn't give you much in the way of moral guidance.

You could even say that life began at the moment that matter was created by the Big Bang, because the process certainly began there.

But if you mean: does life begin at fertilisation, or at cell separation or at the first quickening in the womb or at the moment of birth when the new creature has independent life then you are asking, for the purposes of morality, the wrong question.

The proper question is: When do I (that is you, not Me) incur a moral responsibility for this life? And there is no clear-cut answer to that question.

You might think that after the moment of birth

the responsibility to safeguard the life at all costs is paramount. While the moral obligations to the sperm, the ovum, the embryo and the foetus may be subject to argument, surely there can be no argument about the obligation to the living, breathing child. But here is a true story told by a moral philosopher:

> Along the Wilderness Road, or Boone's Trail, in the eighteenth century, westward through Cumberland Gap to Kentucky, many families and trail parties lost their lives in border and Indian warfare. Compare two episodes in which pioneers were pursued by savages.
>
> (1) A Scottish woman saw that her suckling baby, ill and crying, was betraying her and her three other children, and the whole company to the Indians. But she clung to her child and they were caught and killed.
>
> (2) A Negro woman, seeing how her crying baby endangered another trail party, killed it with her own hands, to keep silence and reach the fort. Which woman made the right decision?[3]

You see, even the sanctity of life of a living, breathing human being may be a qualified condition. And even while still *in utero* the right of the foetus to protection is not unqualified. Here is another story from the same philosopher:

> Several years ago Congress passed a special bill giving citizenship to a Roumanian Jewish doctor, a woman who had aborted three thousand Jewish women brought to the concentration camp. If pregnant, they would have been incinerated. Even accepting the view that the embryos were 'human lives' (which many of us do not), by 'killing' three thousand the doctor saved three thousand and prevented the murder of *six thousand*![4]

---

[3] Joseph Fletcher, *Situation Ethics*, SCM Press, London, 1966, p 124
[4] *ibid*, p 133

But here is an even knottier problem for those who are worried about when it is that life begins or acquires the prerogatives of protection.

> When a lady in Arizona learned, a few years ago, that she *might* bear a defective baby because she has taken thalidomide, how was she to decide? She asked the court to back her doctor in terminating the pregnancy, and it refused, to the judge's chagrin, since the law prohibits nonmedically indicated abortions without exception. Her husband took her to Sweden, where love has more control of law, and there she was aborted. God be thanked, since the embryo was hideously deformed.[5]

You will appreciate, I am sure, that the editorialising about love, law and Me being thanked was done by Joseph Fletcher, not Me. However, let's contemplate the ethical issues involved in this last story.

Would it not have been better to wait until the child was born, just to be absolutely certain that it was deformed, and then kill it? The abortion was a gamble. The other way would be a certainty.

You can't be serious?

Why not?

Well, there is something special that happens at the moment of separation of mother and child.

True. But what happens is that your *perception* of the creature is changed, because you can more easily identify with a baby you can see than with an embryo or foetus which you cannot see. But logically it makes more sense, if you are going to cut the thread of life, to do it when you can see clearly what you are doing.

Let me put another matter to you.

Suppose that the baby had been born deformed and

---

[5] *ibid*, p 135

with a poor prognosis for quality and length of life. Indeed, left for nature to take its course the baby would die within a few hours. But given the possibilities inherent in medicine which can defeat nature, the baby could be kept alive for years. The question then arises: to unnaturally prolong life or to let nature have its way? What should be done?

Personally, I would let nature take its course.

All right then. Who should have the right to make that decision?

The parents, I suppose. They are the ones who will have to live with the consequences of the choice.

Ah, but it is an important principle of law that life and death decisions should be made by disinterested judges. We should not permit those who have a vested interest in the consequences of a decision to make that decision themselves.

Well, then I suppose that the doctors should make the choice. Or a hospital ethics committee.

But then you have people making the choice who do not have to live with the consequences of their own decisions. They say: 'Let the baby live.' And from that point on they have no further responsibility for it. They don't have to live with it, or visit it, or pay for its health care. You would have to suspect that the disinterested doctor or ethics committee lacks due seriousness in making the decision. It's not good enough.

Okay. Who, then, is fit to make the decision?

Don't ask Me. I'm only God. I merely offer this little moral exercise as another example of how impossible it is to make hard and fast rules about where life begins, who has the right to end it and in what circumstances.

One of the most tantalising trick moral questions is the one that supposes you to be in a burning room with da Vinci's *Mona Lisa* and a baby. You can only save one. Which do you choose? The unique painting or the baby, of which there are more than enough in the world?

That's an easy one. I would save the baby any day.

All right. Think about this. You are in the same burning room with the *Mona Lisa* and a baby chimpanzee. Which do you save? The unique painting or the animal with which you share all but 2 per cent of your genes?

Honestly, I don't know.

That's a good answer. Better any day than those who are prepared to say with absolute certainty what they would do. But it doesn't help much in the way of providing watertight rules for behaviour. Even the sanctity of life is a qualified good, as I have already said.

Doctors may struggle valiantly to save the life of a badly deformed and brain damaged baby, even though it has no prospect of a happy or fulfilling life. The same doctors may think nothing of experimenting on a chimpanzee, even when the experiment involves the death of the animal, which left to its own devices could have a very contented chimpy life. Why is the defective human life sacred and the perfect chimp life dispensable?

Joseph Fletcher says that the only reliable guide to how you should make moral choices is love. And the obligations of love will vary from situation to situation—hence the term 'situation ethics'. But that doesn't help much, does it?

Not a lot.

So there you are then. When it comes to matters of life and death all that I can say on the subject is that 'it all depends'. From there you will have to work it out for yourself. And no two situations will be exactly alike.

· 7 ·

Machines & the Future of Humanity

You said some time ago that You wanted to have something to say on the subject of technology. But before we talk about that, are You a Capitalist or a Socialist?

That's about as silly as asking Me if I am male or female. But as we have already discussed, I make the rain to fall on the just and the unjust and the sun to rise on the good and the evil. So I am, by any definition, a socialist. I give to each according to his needs and expect no more from you creatures than that you act up to the best of your abilities.

Anyway, You said that You wanted to say something about technology . . .

Yes. I have watched the development of machines of extraordinary power and complexity and waited to see some indication that with these improved means at your disposal there would be a sudden flowering of improved ends, as it were. But I see no such thing.

Here you are, able to transmit coloured pictures from anywhere to anywhere on the surface of the planet at the instant it is happening. This is a wonderful technology. But look at the content. I mean to say, who needs such technology when its chief use seems to be to get the television pictures of the *Miss America* jamboree from America to Australia a few hours quicker than you were able to do by sending the videotape by plane? That's technological progress?

You have technology of extraordinary 'loudness' with which you could say deep and meaningful things to each other—but clearly there is no one around who has anything to say.

Now if satellite transmissions had been available in Beethoven's time the whole world could have shared in the premier performance of the ninth symphony. Except that the available evidence suggests that if satellite television transmissions had been available in 1823 Beethoven wouldn't have written the ninth symphony. He would have been a rock 'n' roll performer. Rather than writing music of genius he would have been a buffoon—a parody or a perversion of a musician.

This is truly perplexing. Beethoven had no fax machine, no internal combustion or jet engine, no heavier-than-air flying machines or television or photocopiers. Yet he wrote the nine great symphonies which will be performed for as long as human civilisation flourishes. Now name one creation of the age of satellite television that will be heard or seen in 170 years time. Is there one?

Shakespeare didn't even have a typewriter, yet is there one play currently being written on a word processor that will have audiences enthralled in the year 2384— as far in the future as Shakespeare is in the past? How to explain this paradox that technology seems to kill creativity?

Has television produced anything that will merit preservation? Now and then it produces a flash of gold amongst the dross, but it produces such a tolerance for dross that you are in danger of losing your powers of discrimination.

Perhaps it is the fact that technology makes life so easy that kills inspiration. Here is an interesting story which has the makings of a parable:

> Hounded by the KGB and the Communist Party, novelist Mikhail Berg for years eked out a meagre living tending a steam boiler, writing at night the books he knew the state would never publish.
>
> When democracy and freedom came to Russia he emerged from the underground to found a St Petersburg literary journal. His art at last saw the light of day.
>
> Now Berg is nostalgic for the good old days of Soviet repression. 'The feeling of inner freedom and inner righteousness then was incomparable to what we have now,' Berg said in an interview. 'On the surface intellectuals can't help but support what is happening today. But the whole intelligentsia shares a feeling of loss, uneasiness and nostalgia.'
>
> Lev Timofeyev, a writer and former political prisoner, went one step further in describing the new situation in which writers and poets no longer confront a repressive government. 'The intelligentsia has ceased to exist in the form that it existed for the past 200 years in Russia . . . There is no longer a historical need for it.'
>
> Many intellectuals and artists are appalled by the triumph of material values. The joy of freedom of speech has given

way to the cacophony of Avon ads and MTV videos. Their children lust after BMWs and they wonder if this is what they struggled for during the dark years of totalitarianism.[1]

Could Beethoven have written the music to the Ode to Joy, all about freedom and universal brotherhood, had it not been for the fact that he was living under an absolute monarchy and longing for something that did not yet exist? It's a moot point.

What are You suggesting—that we are happier when we are miserable?

Not happier, but certainly more creative. No—I am simply observing that technology and creativity, except in the narrowest mechanical spheres of computer chips and double overhead camshaft internal combustion engines, do not seem compatible.

And also that as the technological means improve the content diminishes. So powerful, earth-moving means now serve the most banal, wretched and worthless of ends. And sometimes the most inhumane and destructive of ends. It is a truism to say, as has been said by a philosopher of media, that 'every new technology demands a new war'. But it is true, nevertheless—in spite of its obviousness.

What should we do? Play the Luddite and smash the machines?

No, of course not. But you should seriously consider the possibility that you are a civilisation in decline and that in a curious and paradoxical way it is your mastery of technology that has brought you down.

Survival in a harsh and brutal environment where life is short requires a type of discipline that is not needed in an easy environment where machines do the work

---

[1] *Guardian Weekly,* London, 2 August 1992

and life is long and relatively free of external stress. In such an easy environment you do not need to teach your children the lessons of discipline. So they become soft and self-indulgent.

Children who survive in a harsh environment will probably have a high level of self-restraint that is imparted to them by their mothers, for their own good. Children of the soft environment may be no match for the barbarians who discipline their children harshly.[2]

So what can we do about it?

Nothing, it would seem. We will just have to wait and see what the outcome is going to be, won't we? But you can't help but be impressed by the difference between the Russian intelligentsia under various tyrants and what passes for intellectual activity in the West.

Berg and Timofeyev had the most limited technology at their disposal—at the best a clandestine printing press, at the most meagre they were reduced to whispers. Yet the content of their media was a great clash of ideas. Liberty itself was at stake.

You have the most powerful media technologies imaginable and the content is nothing more than petty whingeing or banal thumpings that are misnamed 'music'. There must be some lesson to be derived from the inverse relationship of the power of the medium to the value of the content.

I suppose we should thank Me that Beethoven never had a mobile phone. He would never have knuckled down to putting all those dots onto the paper that by a wonder of physics can be transformed into sounds which transport us to the heavens. Where, of course, I already Am!

In fact, had he had a fax and a mobile phone in his

---

[2] The idea of 'restraint' and the rise and fall of civilisations is the central thesis in *The Hungry Ape* by Dr Jim Penman (self-published).

car I suppose that he would have rung up Schubert and Weber and formed a rock group called the *Wiener Schnitzels*. And they would have made video clips for MTV and been patronised by gormless presenters in funny hats. And made lots of money. And still have gone deaf, but for different reasons.

My Me, this is a disappointing age.

Well, on that somewhat dismal note I am afraid that we have to leave it for today. Probably for this era, for that matter. It has been a great pleasure talking to God today. Thank You very much for Your time.

Not at all. The pleasure has been all Mine.

Perhaps we could do this again some time?

We could, if you're still there. I will be, of course, but it is by no means a foregone conclusion that you will be. If you are not very careful your technology will eat you. And I will be very interested to see what takes your place. Cockroaches, I've been told. That's not a very attractive prospect, is it?

So My last word to you is: take care! You are on your own down there. Don't come whingeing to Me when you mess things up. Any creature that can fit Beethoven's ninth in stereophonic sound on one side of a 12 centimetre record ought to be grown-up enough to take responsibility for its own future.

Your Almightyship—once again, thank You.

· 8 ·

Omega

W̱hen I was a young man—a mere boy, really—and
a theological student at the Churches of Christ College
of the Bible, I had a disturbing experience.

As part of our course in pastoral studies (Practical
Church Work, I think it was called officially) our class
visited the Kew Cottages in Melbourne.

At that time (*c*1960), the cottages were home to people
with all sorts of mental disabilities. In some parts of
the establishment there were people with severe psych-
oses who were deluded and violent. In other parts there
were children with Down's syndrome who overwhelmed

visitors with both their need for affection and their willingness to give it instantly to strangers.

I knew, vaguely, that the psychotic and the congenitally defective were a part of life's rich tapestry, if you'll pardon the cliché. What I was not prepared for was a ward full of hydrocephalic children with heads so enormous that they were larger than their bodies. These poor creatures seemed to have absolutely no awareness that there was anything going on around them, although the nurses assured us that they could respond to small kindnesses.

Nevertheless, these children were so utterly helpless that they could not even move themselves. Their grotesque heads were too huge for their tiny muscles to move. The nurses had to turn them over from time to time, as well as do everything else for them.

I learned two things that day. The first was that there are wonderful human beings who every day go to work to perform tasks that most of us would try to avoid at all costs. They seemed to me to go beyond the expectations of duty or patience and to actually put an extra quality into their work. Is it fanciful to call it 'love'? I don't know. But I do know that they are unsung heroes of our society. They will never be rich or be awarded Orders of Australia precisely because we do not want to know what it is that they do every day. How can you give an Order of Australia to someone with the citation: 'For services to humanity, but we would rather not say what services?'

The second thing I learned was this. Never to be too glib about affirmations of belief.

After spending a morning in these disturbing environments we young, would-be men-of-God had a session with one of the resident doctors. The first words he said to us, while we were clearly still in a state of shock from what we had seen, were: 'Gentlemen, do you still believe in God?'

Could God have done this? Or permitted it? Was God not looking when it happened? Did someone sin, that the punishment for the fathers' sins should be visited in such a horrible way on the children? Does anyone really believe that there is some ineffable system of divine justice that proceeds by punishing the children for the sins of the fathers? By human standards it is too monstrous to entertain for a moment. So what mental gymnastics are required to imagine a God who *permits* (if that is the right word) such calamities?

Perhaps it was on that day at Kew Cottages that the seed of the new agnostic theology was planted in my mind. Yes. There may be a God, but if there is then it is clear that She does not take a very close interest in what is going on on this planet. It is simply not possible to imagine a morally attractive deity with infinite powers, infinite knowledge and infinite mercy permitting such things to happen.

It was clear to me that day that some things just happen. One day we will understand what goes wrong in the development of the embryo which lays the grotesque foundations for such a disaster. Then we will be able to correct such abnormalities *in utero*. As with smallpox, polio, German measles and every other disease that flesh is prone to, we human beings will fix it up ourselves.

If we truly believed that such things are the will of God, then we would have to agree with Pope Leo XII that it is impious to interfere and obstruct His will, as Leo believed about the iniquity of smallpox vaccination.

But it is not the will of God. I can't prove that that is the case—but I don't need to. It is axiomatic. If the Life Force is indeed responsible for such crimes then we should not worship it, we should kill it.

And there are no miracles. To even suggest that there are is too monstrous a moral concept to entertain for a nanosecond.

There is no escaping the conclusion that everything that happens on this planet happens by an inexorable process of cause and effect. If we had all the information at our disposal there is nothing that could not be explained in terms of physics and chemistry, including the emergence of life itself four billion years ago.

Sometimes chance enters into the equation. It is simply bad luck to give birth to a deformed child. There is nothing at all that can be said that will make sense of such an event. It may well bring forth wonderful qualities in certain people who come into contact with the child, but to suggest that the Life Force intentionally planned such an event to test someone's Christian charity is an appalling calumny on the Creator, if there is One.

In the end we don't *need* God. God is a completely useless concept. We come into the world; we fill in some time; we return to the earth; ashes to ashes, dust to dust.

'In sure and certain hope of life everlasting'?

Four billion years ago the first self-replicating molecules emerged from the primeval soup. That beginning is like one end of a thread of life which presumably will stretch off into the future as far ahead as it reaches into the past. I am a tiny strand in that, what to all intents and purposes, is the thread of eternal life.

Did Something will this into being? I have no idea. Finally, there is not much more that can be said on the subject than has been said by physicist Paul Davies:

> The very fact that the universe *is* creative, and that the laws have permitted complex structures to emerge and develop to the point of consciousness—in other words, that the universe has organised its own self-awareness—is for me powerful evidence that there is 'something going on behind it all'.[1]

It would be exciting to be around in four billion years time to see if anything has happened in the meantime that has settled the questions of Meaning and Purpose once and for all.

---

[1] Paul Davies, *The Cosmic Blueprint*, Heinemann, London, 1987, p 203

Bibliography

Bainton, Roland, *Here I Stand—a Life of Martin Luther*, Abingdon Press, New York, 1960

Brown, R Hanbury, *The Wisdom of Science*, Cambridge University Press, Cambridge, 1986

Davies, Paul, *The Cosmic Blueprint*, Heinemann, London, 1987, *The Mind of God*, Simon & Schuster, New York, 1992

Dawkins, Richard, *The Blind Watchmaker*, Longman Cheshire, London, 1986, *The Selfish Gene*, Oxford University Press, Oxford, 1976

Fletcher, Joseph, *Situation Ethics*, SCM Press, London, 1966

God, *The Bible—Revised Standard Version*, Thomas Nelson & Sons, New York, 1946 and 1952 editions

Kahl, Joachim, *The Misery of Christianity*, Pelican, Melbourne, 1968

Nigg, Walter, *The Heretics—Heresy Through the Ages*, Dorset, London, 1949

Penman, Jim, *The Hungry Ape*, Self-published, Melbourne, 1992

Plaidy, Jean, *The Spanish Inquisition*, Robert Hale, London, 1978

Smith, Warren Sylvester (ed), *Shaw on Religion*, Constable, London, 1967

Tuchman, Barbara, *A Distant Mirror*, Macmillan, London, 1978

Illustration Sources

p1 Cambridge University Library MS 113, 12; p7 Luther's Bible (September 1522); p28 Staatsbibliothek Munich CLM 4453; p53 Hjalmar Holmquist 'Martin Luther' (1917) p153; p83 Lutherhalle, Wittenberg; p104 Hartmann Schedel, 'Das Buch der Chroniken' (1493); p120 'Les Preaux Gospels—Normandy, late eleventh century'; p126 Geiberg 'Reformation', X, 7.